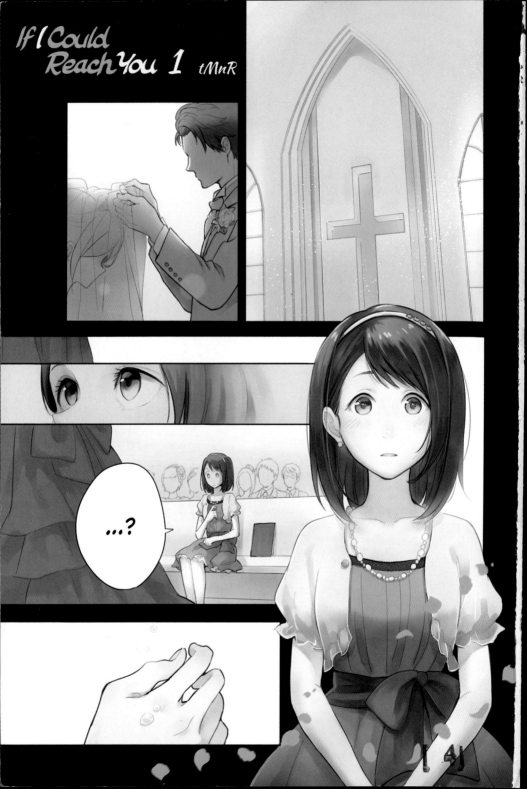

MY
FIRST
CRUSH
BEGAN...

...THE
VERY MOMENT
THAT THE
ONE I LOVED
MOVED
BEYOND
MY REACH.

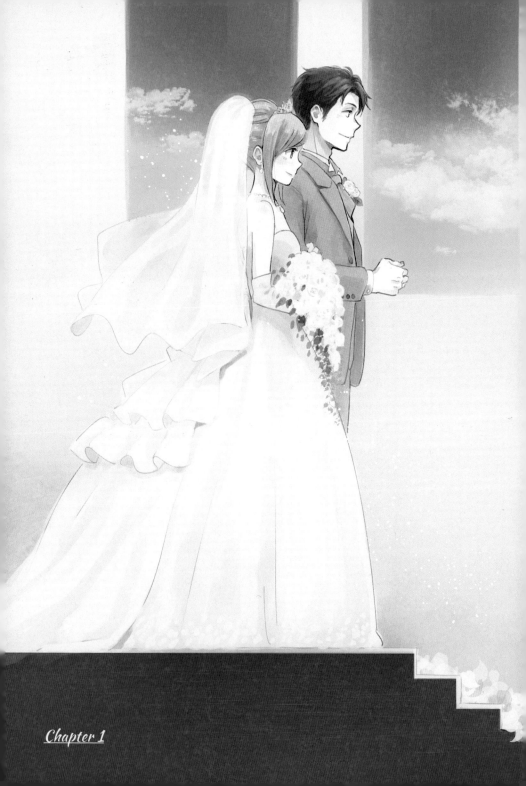

Chapter 1

If I Could Reach You
1

CONTENTS

...

GA-CHK

I'M HOME...

Oh!

WELCOME HOME!

YOU'RE BACK EARLY...

WHAT WERE YOU WORKING ON?

Photos?

I'M SORRY! I'LL GET DINNER STARTED RIGHT AWAY!

ER, WAIT, IT'S ALMOST SUNDOWN?! SINCE WHEN?!

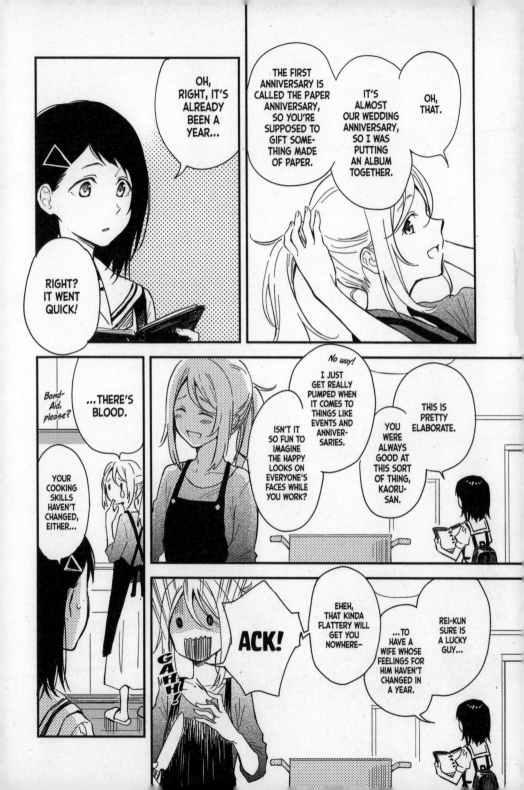

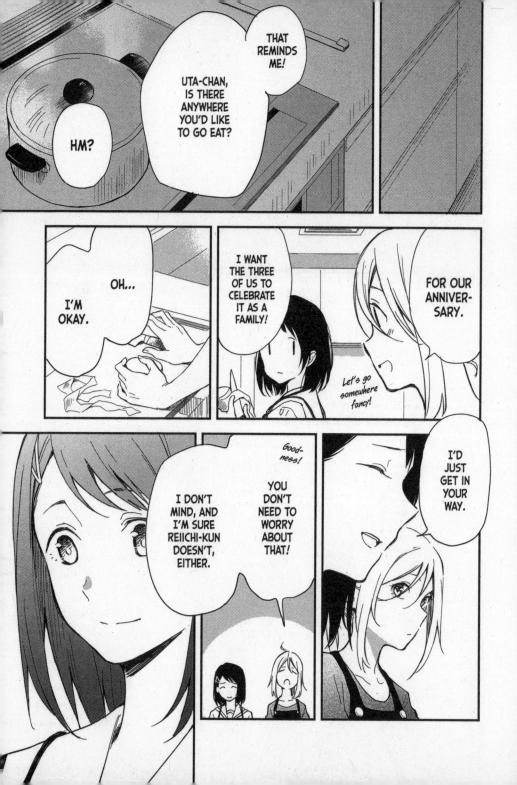

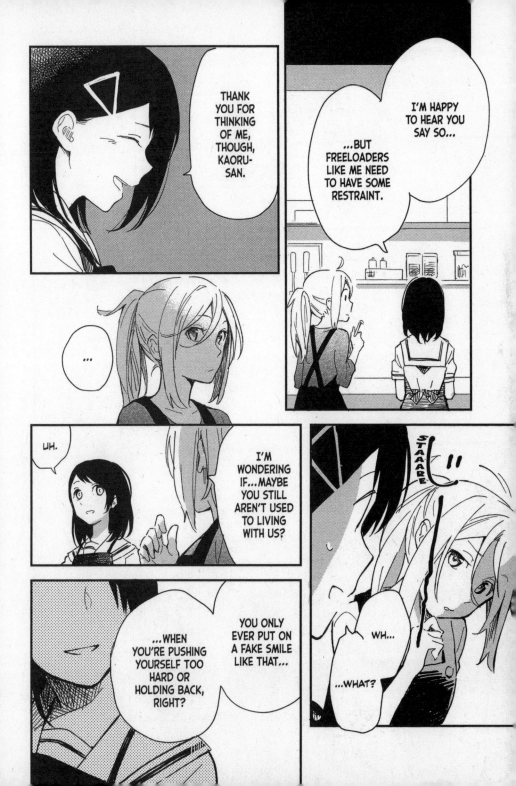

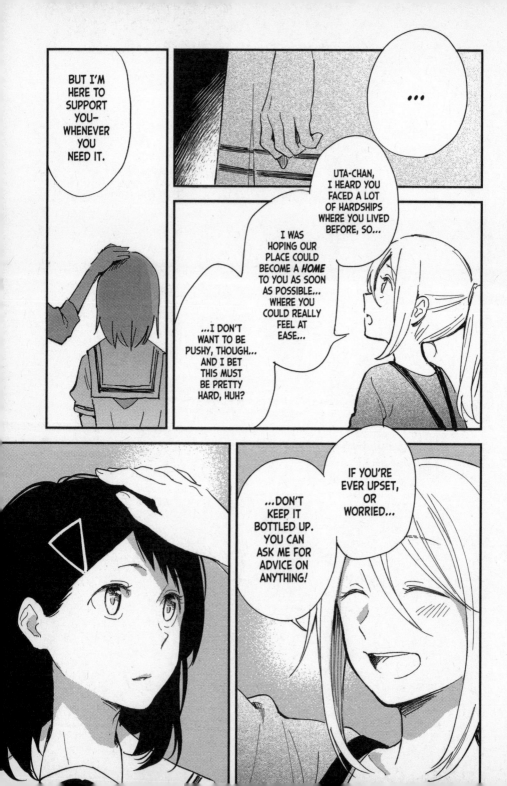

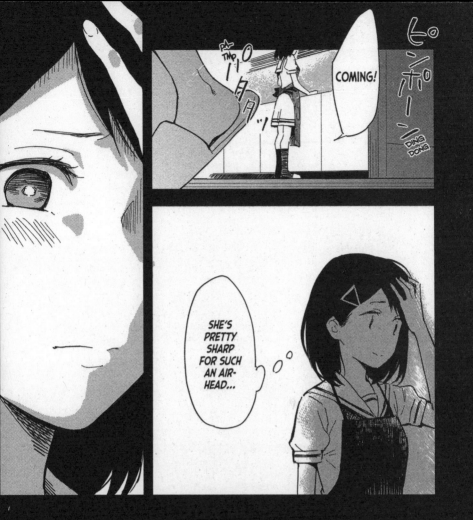

SINCE SHE LIVED NEARBY, AND WAS A FRIENDLY BIG SISTER TO ME, I ALWAYS ADORED HER, TOO...

IT WAS TO HIS CHILDHOOD FRIEND, KAORU-SAN.

ONE YEAR AGO, MY OLDER BROTHER, REI-KUN, GOT MARRIED.

...OR, RATHER, I NEVER NOTICED THAT IT HAD TURNED INTO LOVE— EVEN AS I WATCHED THE TWO GROW CLOSER.

IT WASN'T UNTIL THEIR WEDDING THAT I FINALLY REALIZED...

I WAS STILL SO YOUNG, I HAD NO IDEA THAT WHAT I WAS FEELING WAS LOVE...

THAT DAY WAS WHEN...

...THIS LOVE I COULD NEVER EVEN DREAM TO CONFESS BEGAN.

A ONE-SIDED LOVE... A TOO-LATE LOVE.

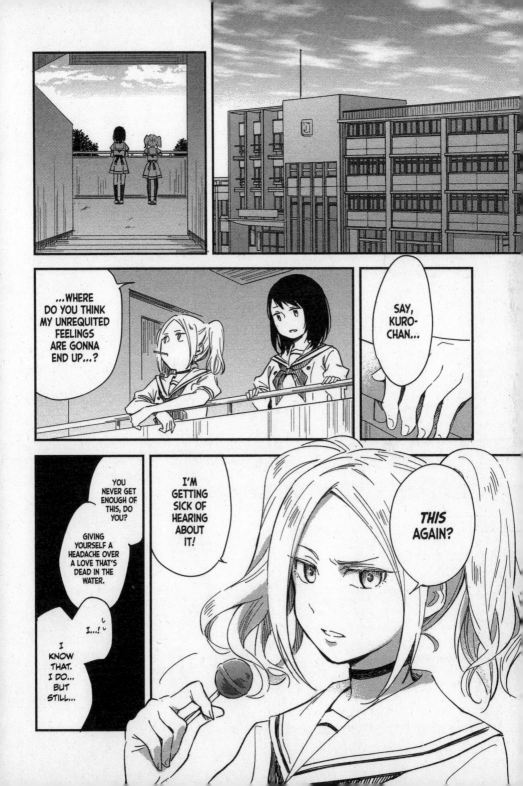

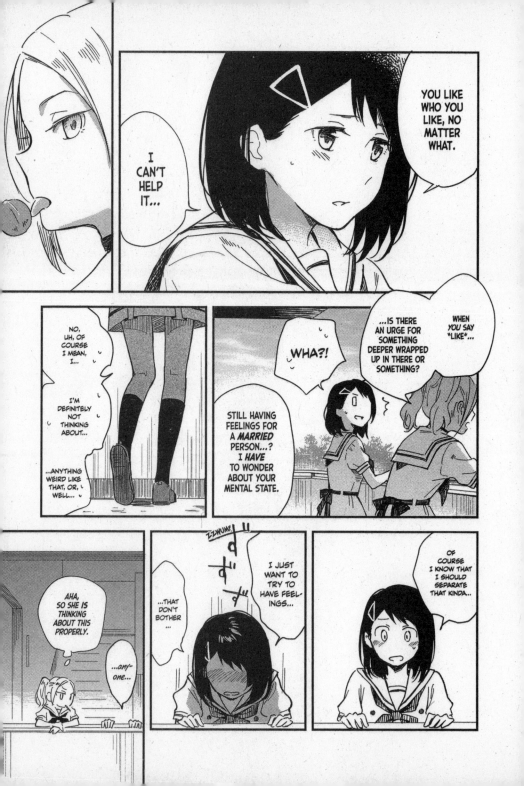

THAT'S A PRETTY RATIONAL RESPONSE...

...FOR SOMEONE WHO'S PLANNING ON CARRYING A RIDICULOUS, UNREQUITED LOVE TO HER GRAVE.

AFTER ALL, LOVE IS A SELFISH THING, Y'KNOW.

BUT I THINK THAT'S WHY YOU'RE STUCK WORRYING ABOUT IT.

WHY NOT JUST FORGET THE SENSIBLE STUFF SOCIETY'S IMPOSED ON YOU, AND CONFESS, OR DO WHATEVER?

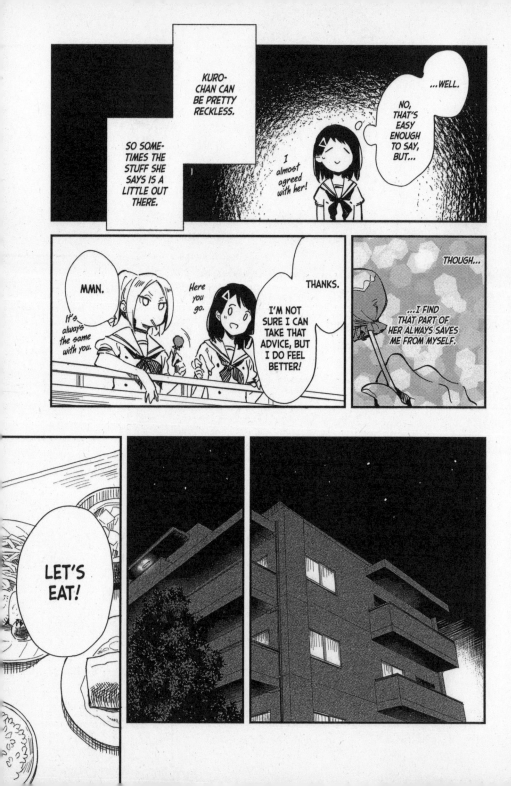

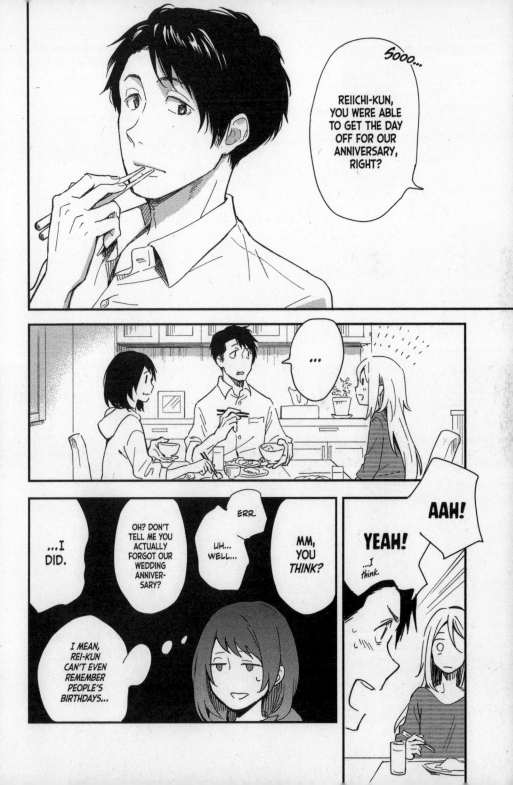

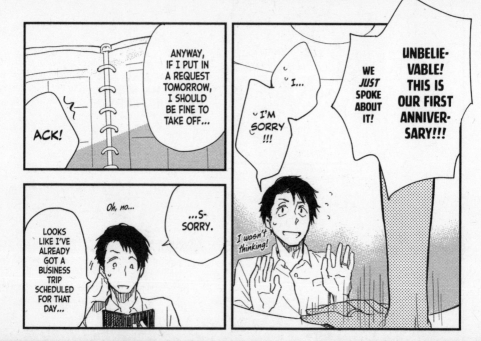

SNAP

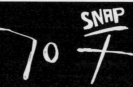

N...NO, I THINK THAT'S SOMETHING NORMAL TO GET ANGRY ABOUT...

I SHOULD SAY SORRY THAT MY BROTHER'S SO INCONSIDERATE.

...SORRY FOR MAKING THINGS WEIRD DURING DINNERTIME...

BROTHER CURRENTLY IN BATH

FSSHH

SIGH...

OF COURSE, NO POINT IN GRIPING TO YOU ABOUT THIS, UTA-CHAN...

...BUT FOR HIM TO NEGLECT EVEN OUR FIRST WEDDING ANNIVERSARY, TOO...

I KNEW FROM THE START THAT HE DIDN'T SWEAT THE DETAILS, AND THAT HE WAS PRETTY BUSY WITH WORK...

...REIICHI-KUN'S BEEN DOING THIS KIND OF THING MORE AND MORE LATELY...

...I GUESS, BUT IT'S MORE LIKE...

CAN I ASK YOU A FAVOR?

SAY, UTA-CHAN!

Y... ...YES?

HMPH

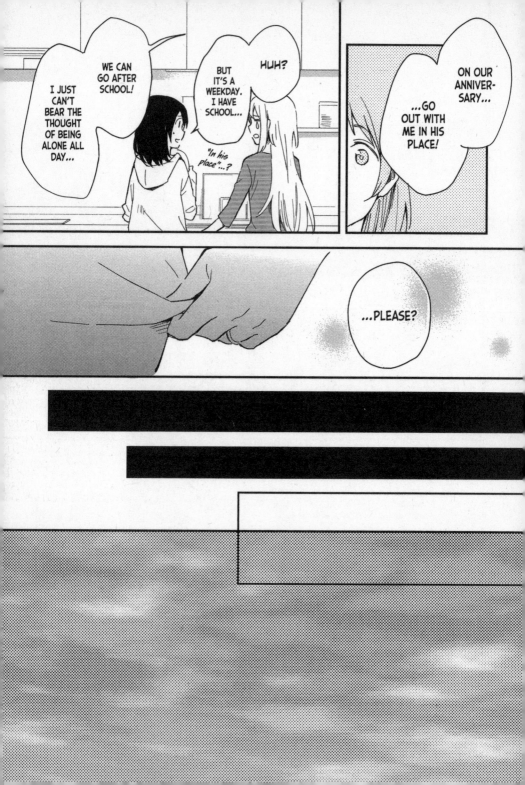

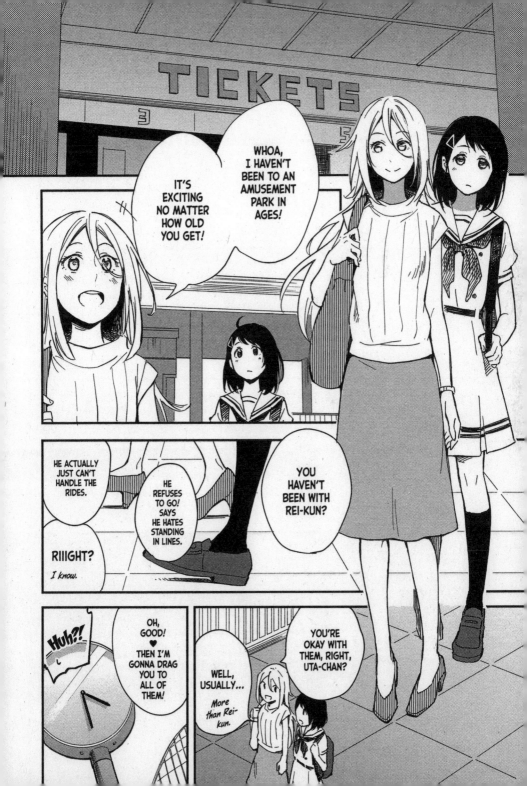

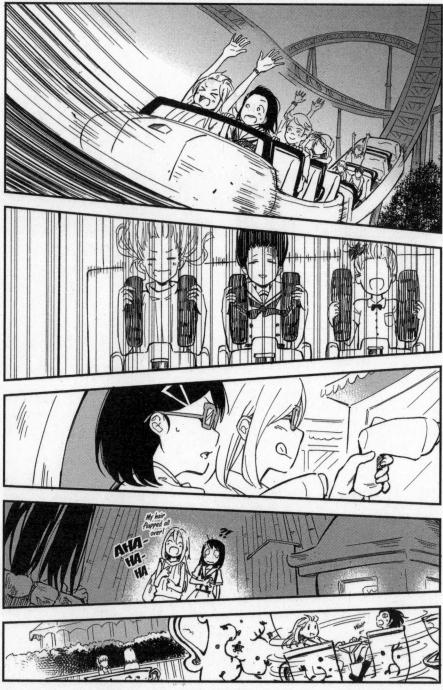

My hair flopped all over!

AHA-HA-HA

?!!

Wait

21

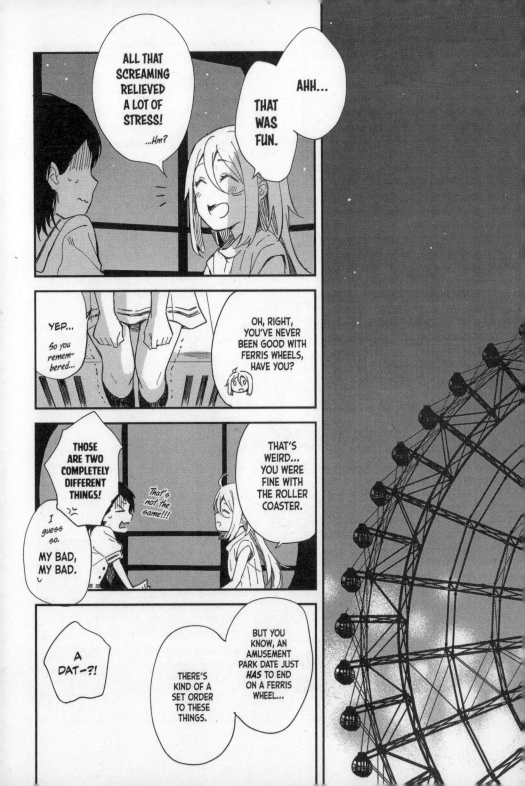

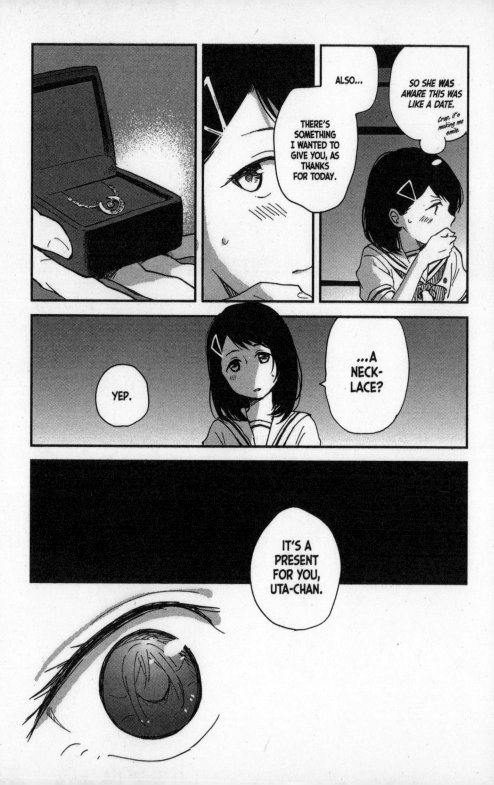

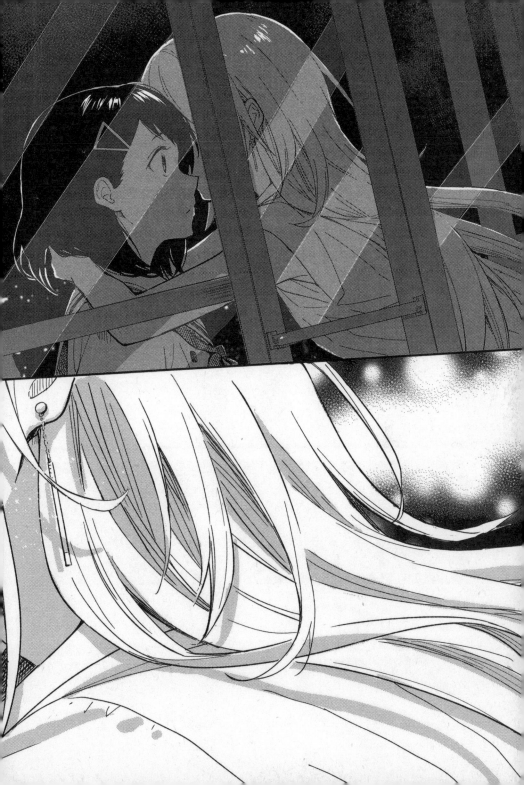

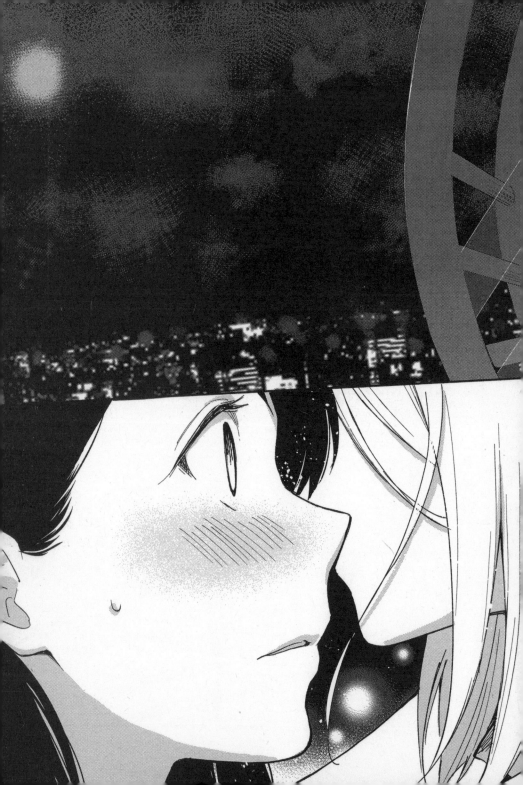

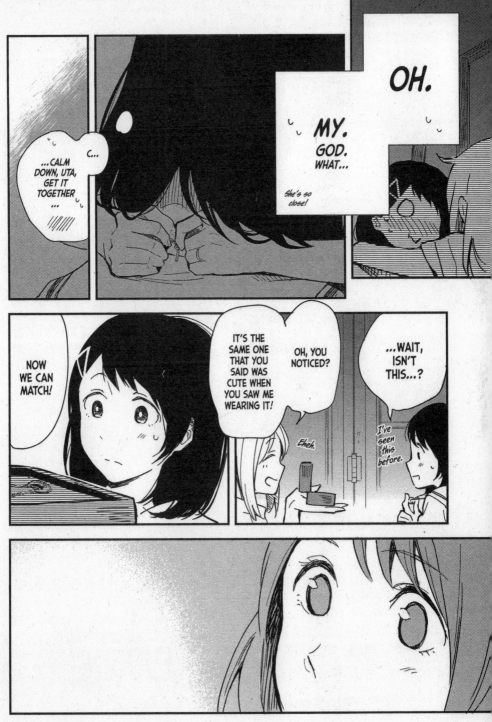

26

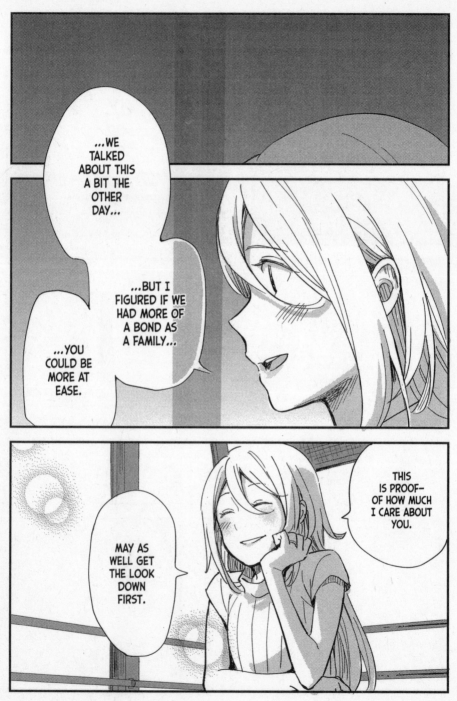

27

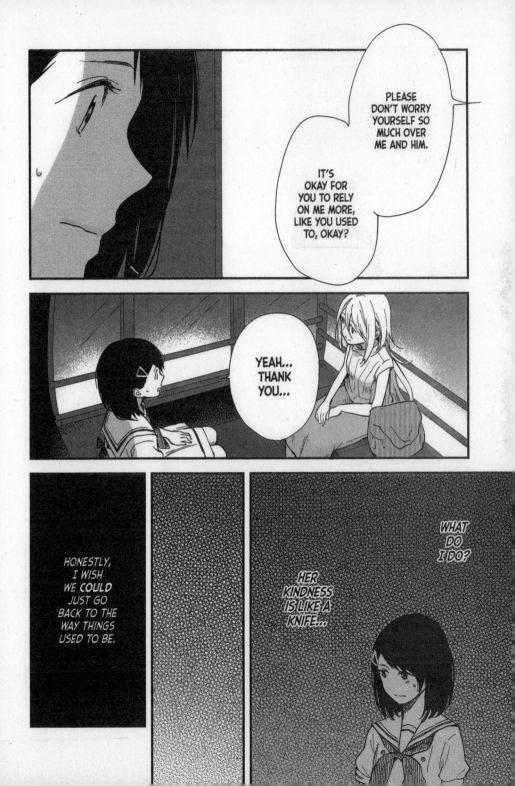

BUT...
...IF I LET MY-SELF FALL FOR THAT KIND OF AFFECTION NOW...
C'MON.
LET'S GO HOME!
It's about to go around again.

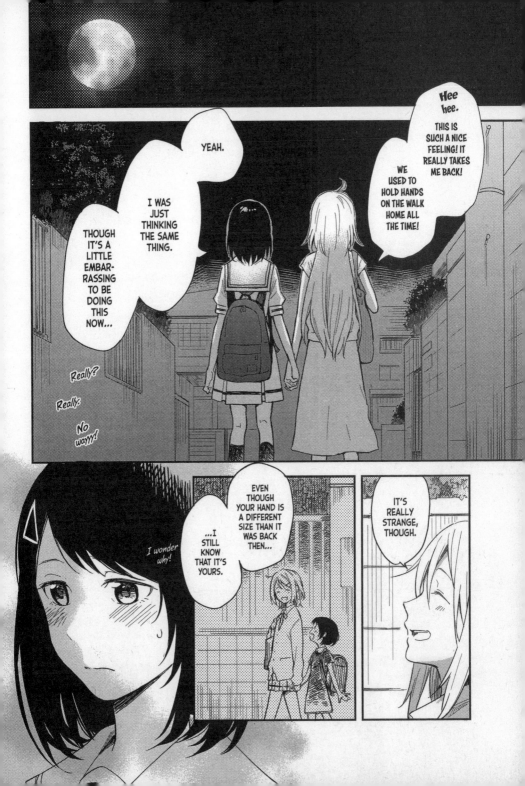

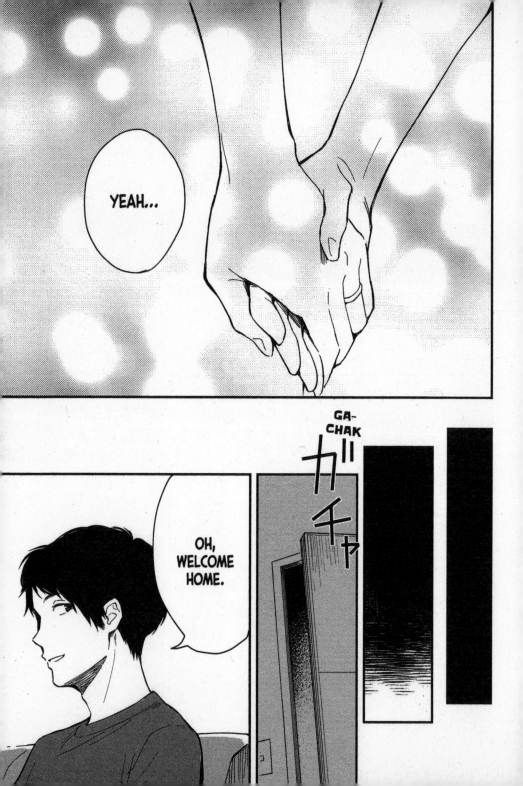

YEAH...

GA-
CHAK

OH,
WELCOME
HOME.

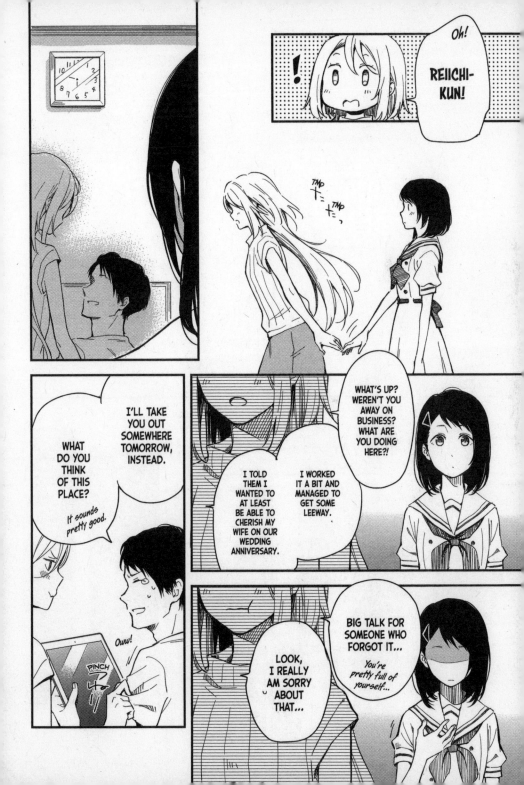

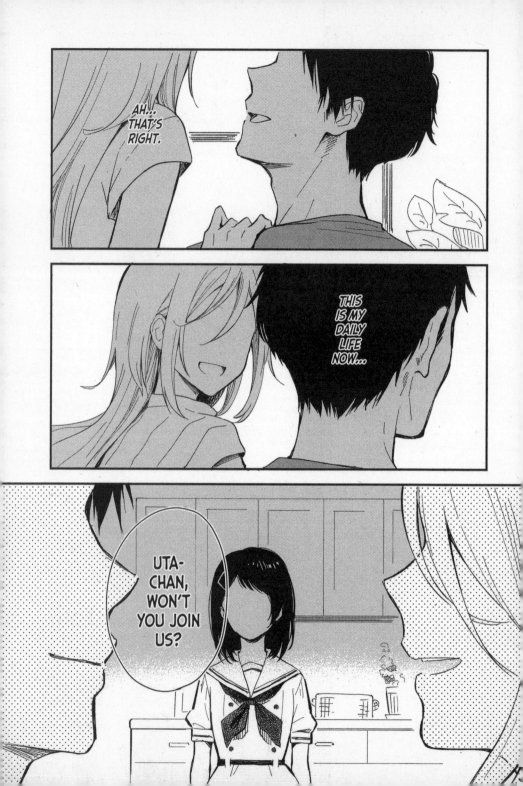

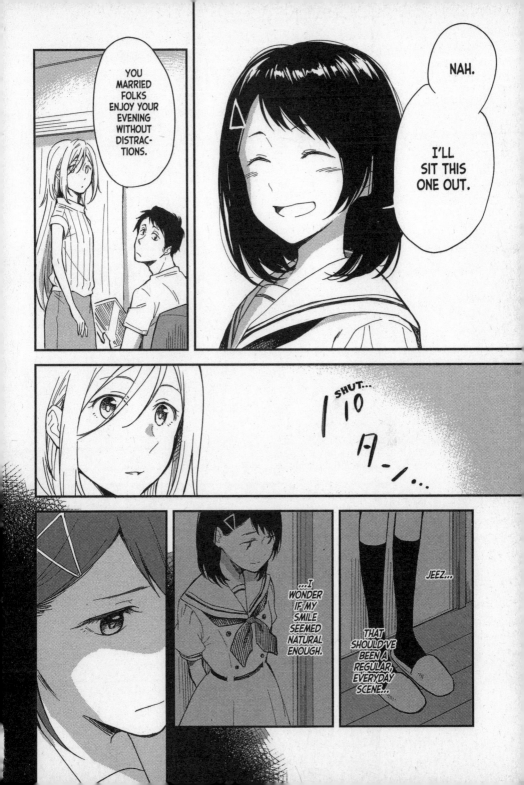

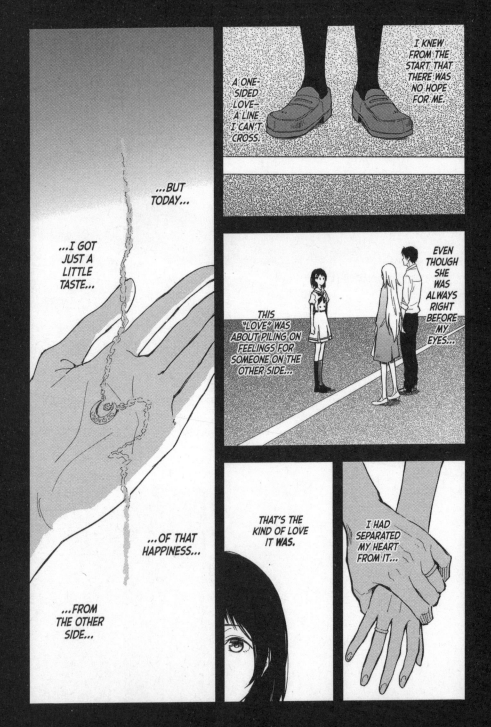

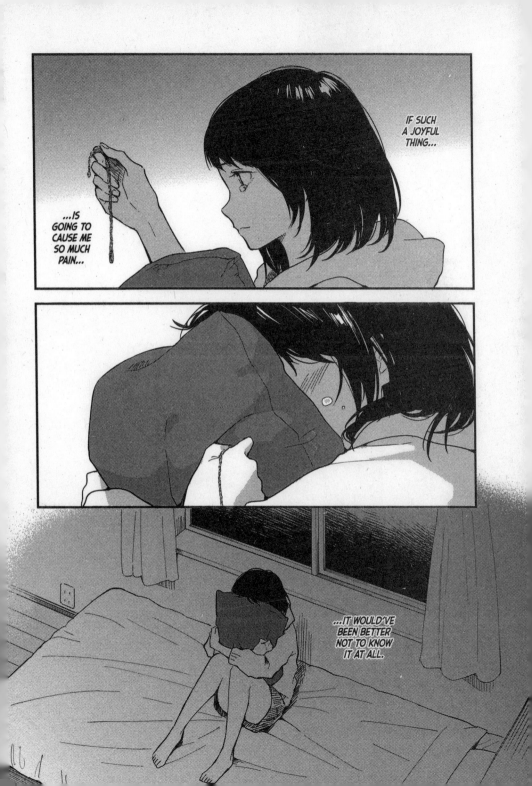

If I Could
Reach You

If I Could
Reach You

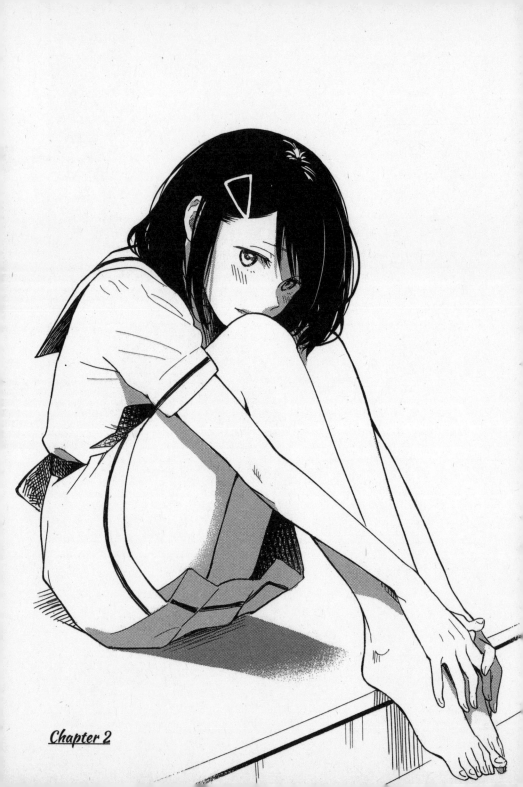

Chapter 2

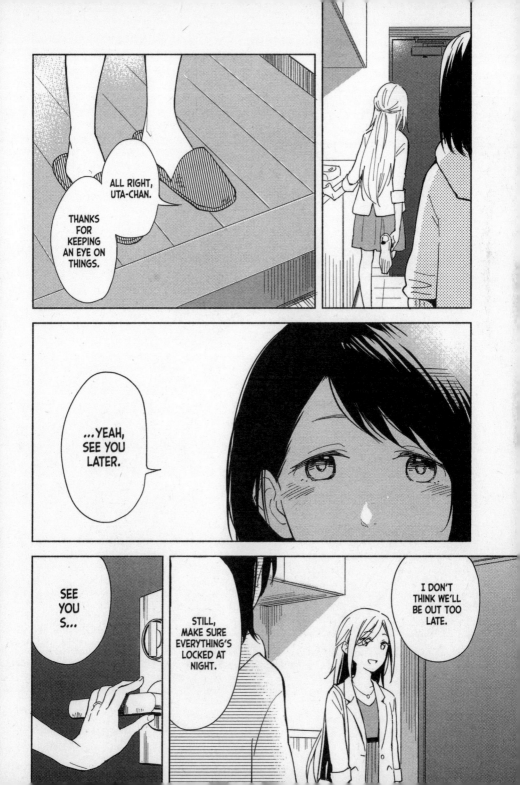

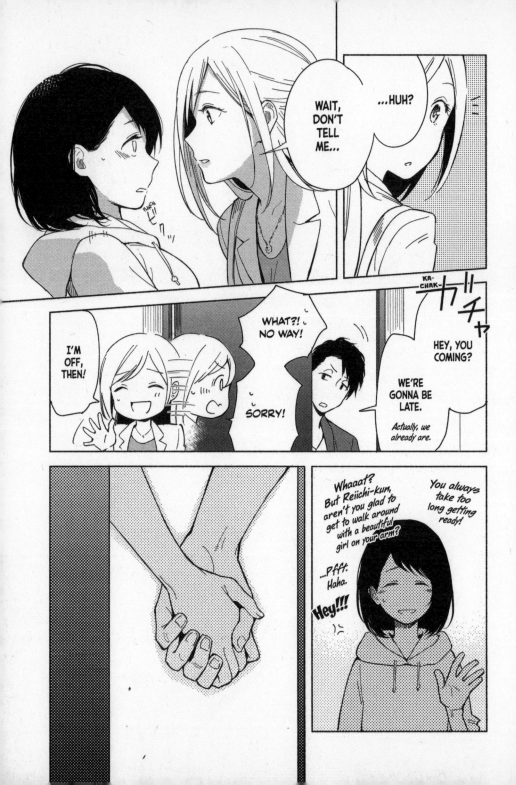

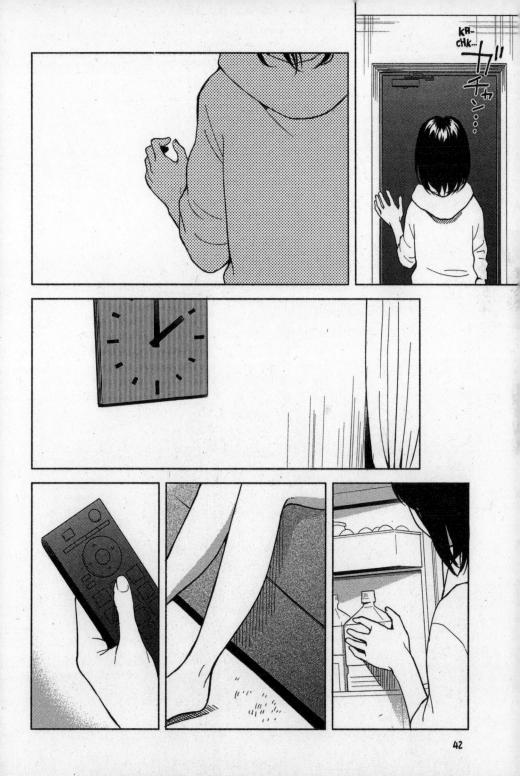

KA-
CHK...

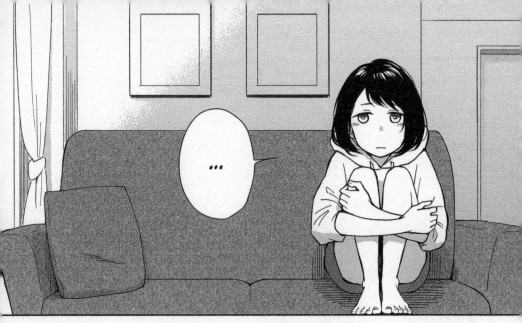

...

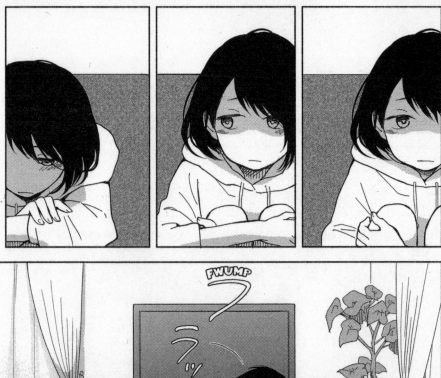

FWUMP

IT'S NO USE.

IT'S DEPRESSING.

THE DESIRES THAT I TOSSED IN THE TRASH HAVE ALL COME SPILLING OUT...

JUST WHEN I ACTUALLY STARTED GETTING USED TO...

...STIFLING MY OWN FEELINGS...

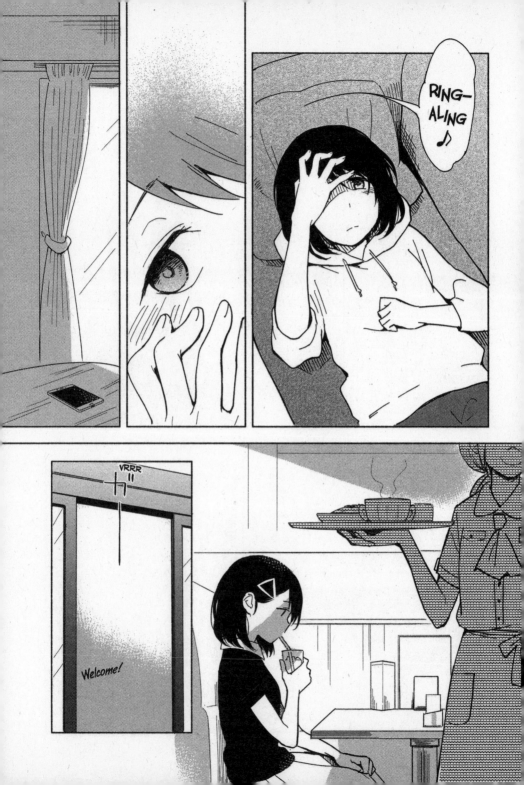

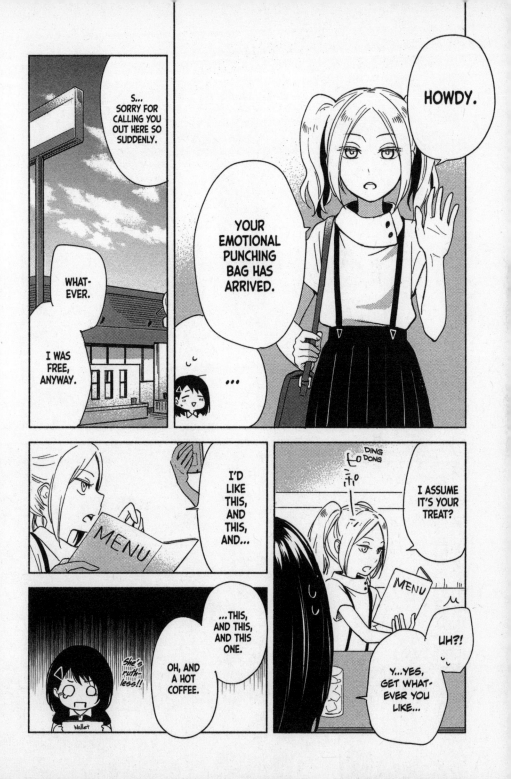

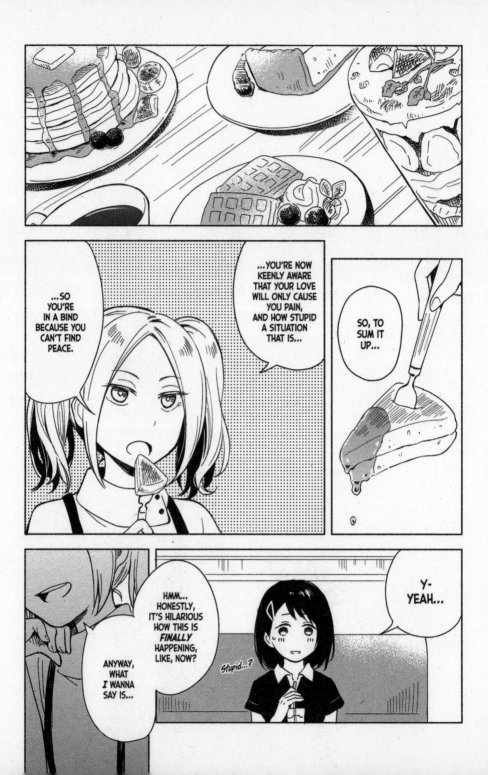

...SINCE THERE'S BEEN SUCH AN INTERESTING DEVELOPMENT...

...I KINDA JUST WANNA GIVE YOU A SHOVE AND SEE YOU SUFFER MORE!

SMIRK

Y'KNOW?!

SHE WOULD...

This is hilarious.

SHE...

WHAT?

After all the talks we've had?

OH, SO EVERYTHING BEFORE *WASN'T* SERIOUS. OKAY.

U... UM...

I REALLY AM SERIOUSLY THINKING THINGS OVER THIS TIME...

TWITCH

CLASSIC KURO-CHAN.

DELIGHTFULLY TWISTED AS ALWAYS...

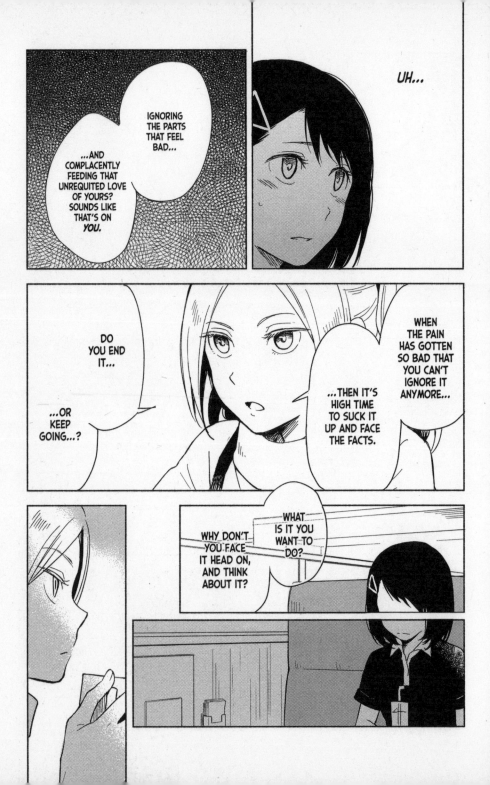

WELL, THAT'S...

...PROBABLY BECAUSE...

DON'T SISTERS-IN-LAW USUALLY HAVE RELATIONSHIPS THAT ARE MORE REMOVED AND ALOOF, ANYWAY?

PLUS...

...ISN'T KAORU-SAN PRETTY OVER-PROTECTIVE OF YOU?

...AND KAORU-SAN...

...FEELS A BIT RESPONSIBLE FOR THAT... I THINK.

...MY PARENTS ARE DIVORCED...

IT'S NO GOOD.

TALKING ABOUT THIS STILL MAKES MY HEAD HURT.

...IT'S KIND OF A LONG STORY, OR, WELL...

...IT'S PRETTY... COMPLI-CATED...

UM...

...HUH? WHAT DO YOU MEAN?

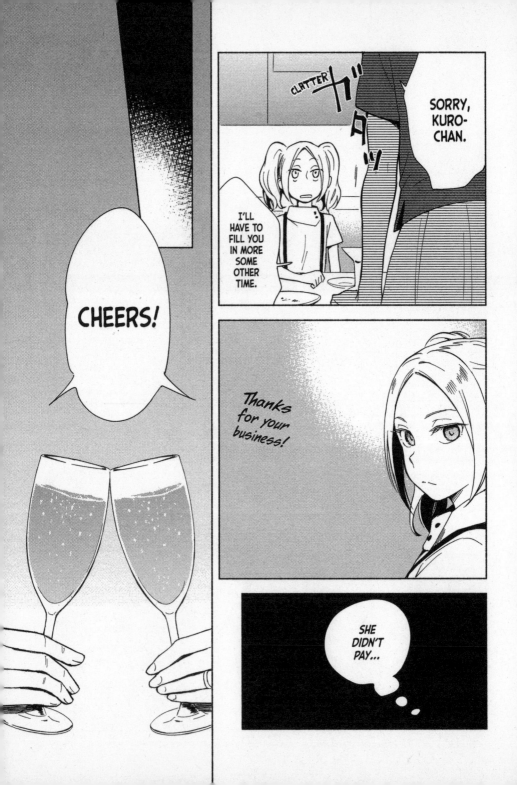

Oh, no!

◇ THIS IS DELICIOUS!

I REALLY DO WISH WE COULD'VE BROUGHT UTA-CHAN ALONG, TOO.

Yumminess is happiness!

NO WAAAY, WHAT IS THIS FLAVOR?

REIICHI-KUN, REIICHI-KUN, THIS IS SOOO GOOD!

I GET IT ALREADY.

Lower your voice!

...HAS GOTTEN HER IN THE HABIT OF NOT RELYING ON ADULTS.

MAYBE HER LIFE UP UNTIL NOW...

THAT'S TRUE. I REALLY WISH SHE WOULD OPEN UP A BIT MORE.

...SHE WASN'T THAT KIND OF KID...

...BACK WHEN I KNEW HER WELL...

...BOTH YOU AND MY MOTHER WERE BY HER SIDE.

BACK THEN...

THINGS CAN CHANGE A LOT IN FIVE YEARS.

I... GUESS SO.

A LOT PROBABLY DID HAPPEN DURING THAT TIME...

...EVEN IF THAT'S TRUE...

...IT DOESN'T CHANGE THE FACT THAT UTA-CHAN GOT HURT IN THE END.

COME ON, STOP LOOKING LIKE YOU BLAME YOURSELF.

THIS ISN'T YOUR FAULT, KAORU.

...IN THAT CASE...

...THERE'S NO NEED TO WORRY.

SO, AT LEAST WHILE WE'RE STILL LIVING TOGETHER...

...I WANT TO MAKE THIS TIME HAPPY FOR HER, IF EVEN JUST A LITTLE BIT.

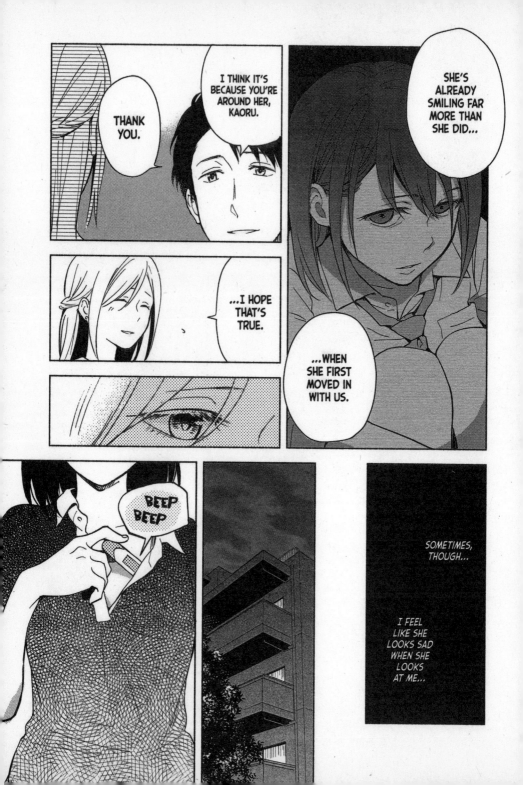

Wah!

COME TO THINK OF IT...

...I WONDER IF THIS WAS WHAT KAORU-SAN WAS TRYING TO TALK TO ME ABOUT BEFORE SHE LEFT...

THAT'S...

38.3°C

...KINDA HIGH...

It's not just a slight fever!

ANYWAY, I NEED SOME MEDICINE...

Where was it?

MMMNN

*AROUND 101°F.

56

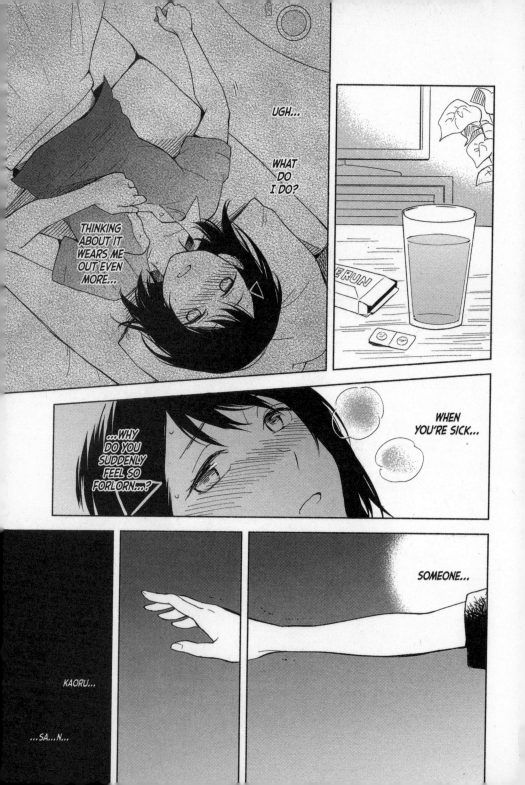

I'M STILL ANNOYED AT YOU, BUT THAT WAS A SURPRISINGLY WELL-PLANNED ANNIVERSARY AGENDA, REIICHI-KUN.

You're so condescending!

WHAT'S IMPORTANT IS THAT YOU ENJOYED IT.

OH!

...

YOU FEELIN' BETTER NOW?

I....

I....

I WASN'T... REALLY ALL THAT MAD, YOU KNOW...

YOU'VE JUST BEEN ACTING KIND OF COLD LATELY, SINCE YOU'VE BEEN PRIORITIZING YOUR WORK SO MUCH.

SO, I...

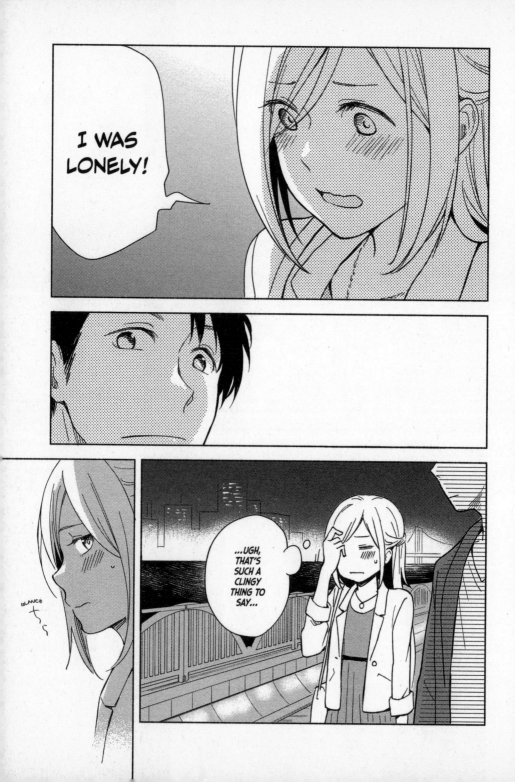

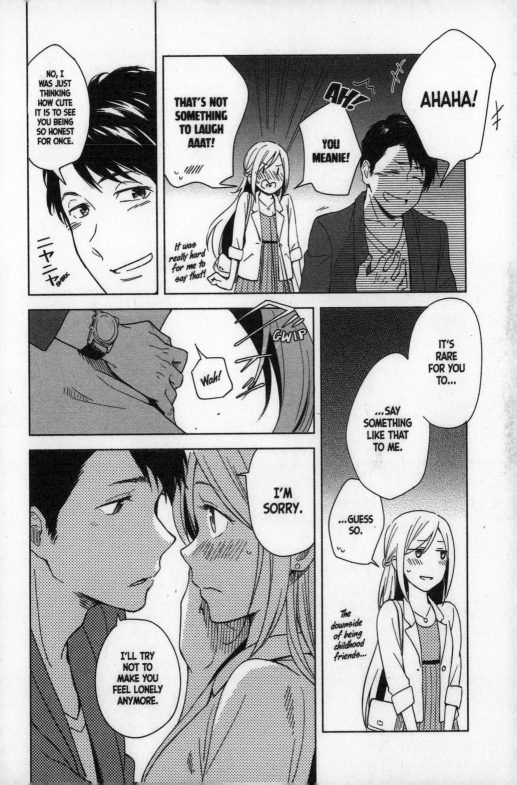

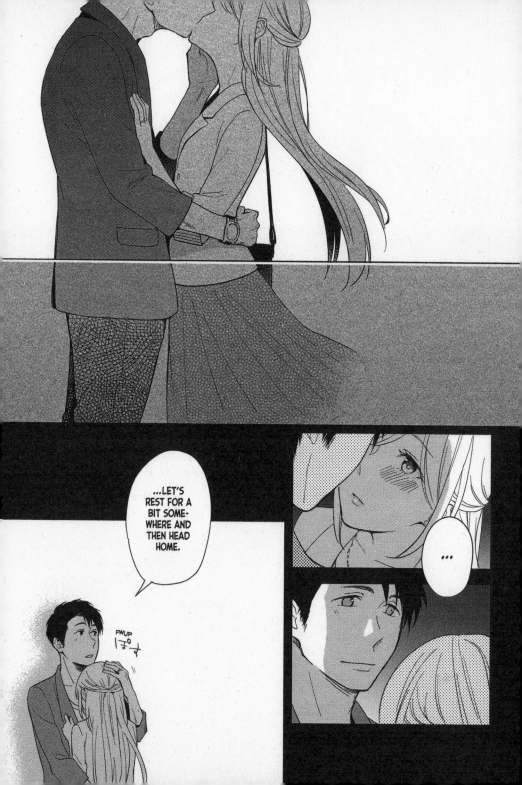

Mm...

AH!

SORRY.

DID I WAKE YOU?

You were crying.

WELL, YOU'RE CLEARLY NOT ALL RIGHT.

YEP! ARE YOU ALL RIGHT?

I can see that.

YEAH...

KAORU...

...SAN...?

62

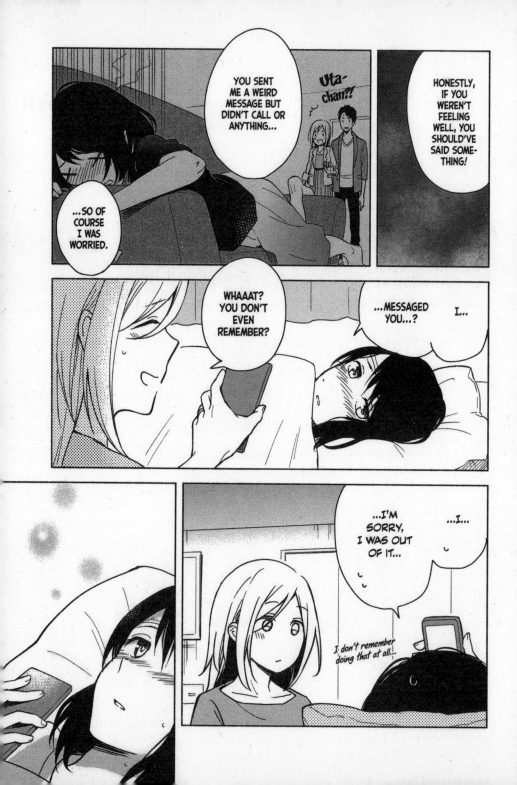

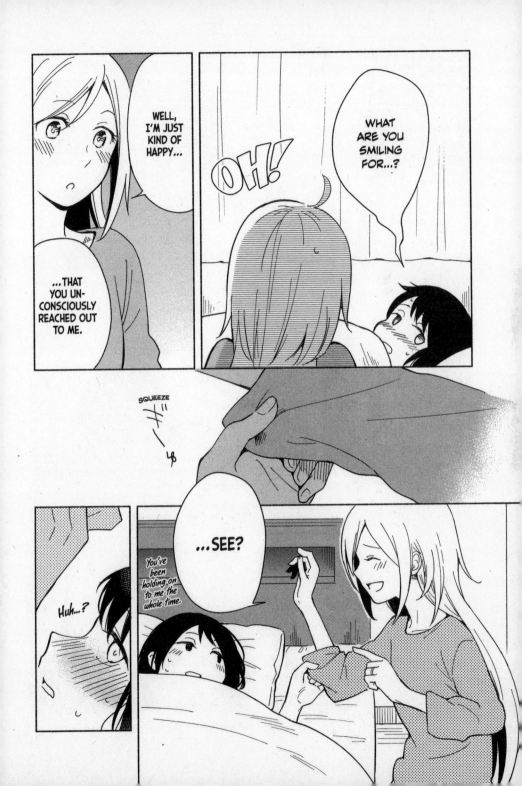

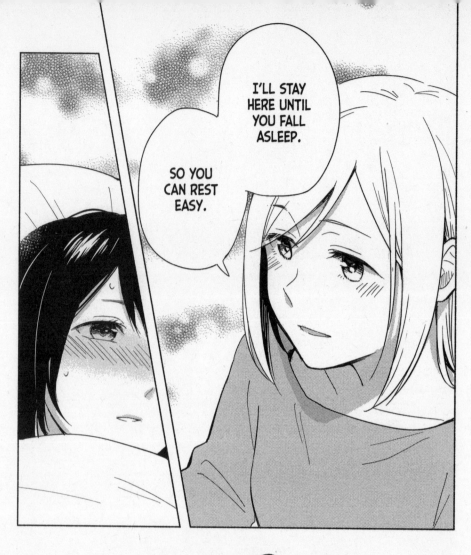
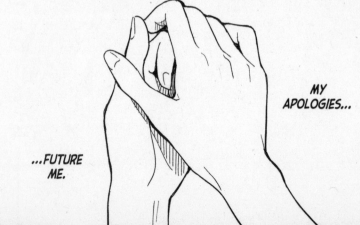

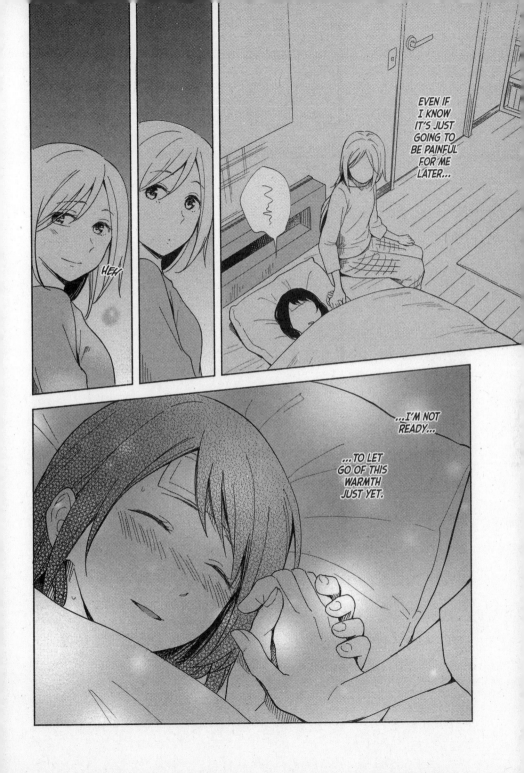

If I Could
Reach You

If I Could
Reach You

Chapter 3

WELL, I DIDN'T EVEN HAVE TO THINK ABOUT WHETHER I WAS NORMAL OR NOT.

ME BEING NORMAL WAS JUST THE DEFAULT.

I THOUGHT THAT I WAS NORMAL.

...

COM-IN'!

REIICHI-KUUUN!

...OR IT SHOULD HAVE BEEN.

G-TUNK

I'M OUT OF BODY WASH! BRING ME SOME FROM UP ON THE SHELF!

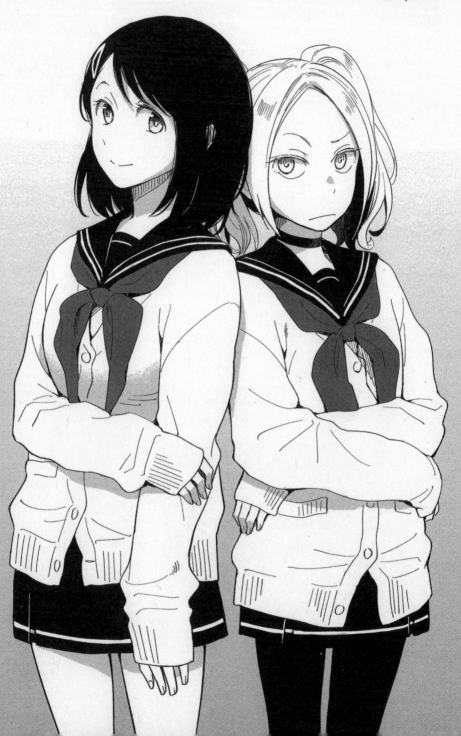

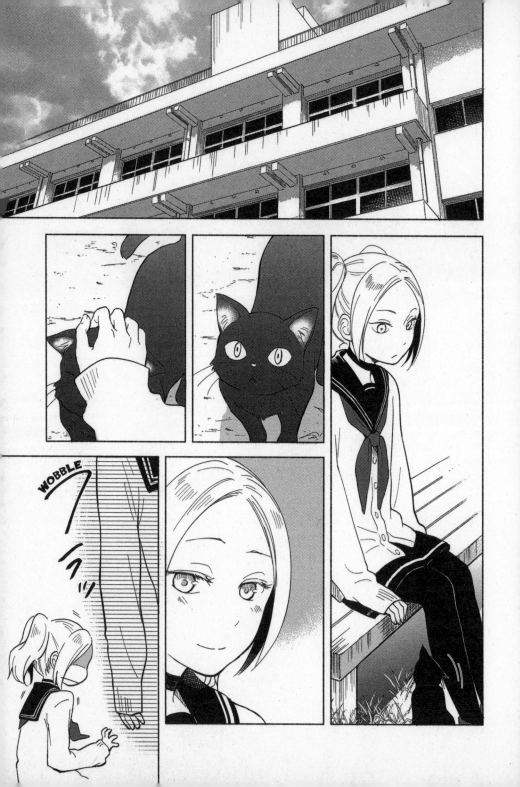

WOBBLE

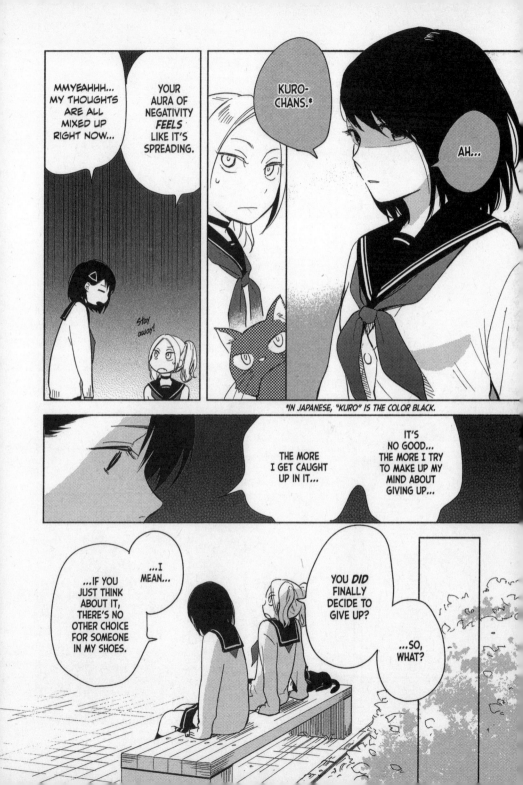

*IN JAPANESE, "KURO" IS THE COLOR BLACK.

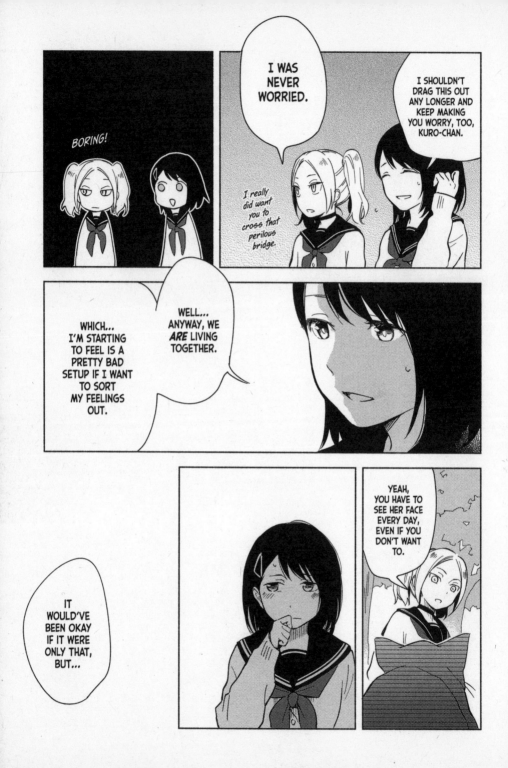

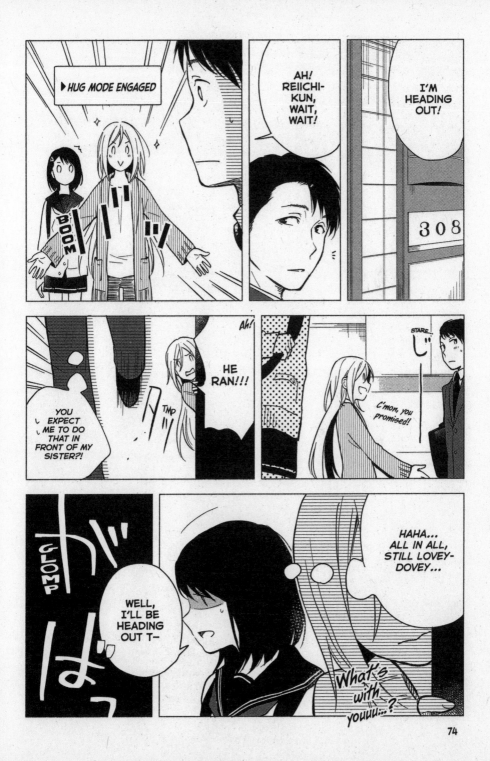

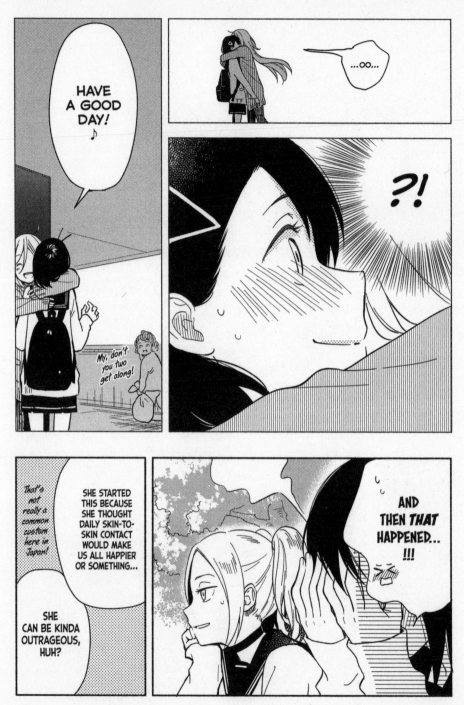

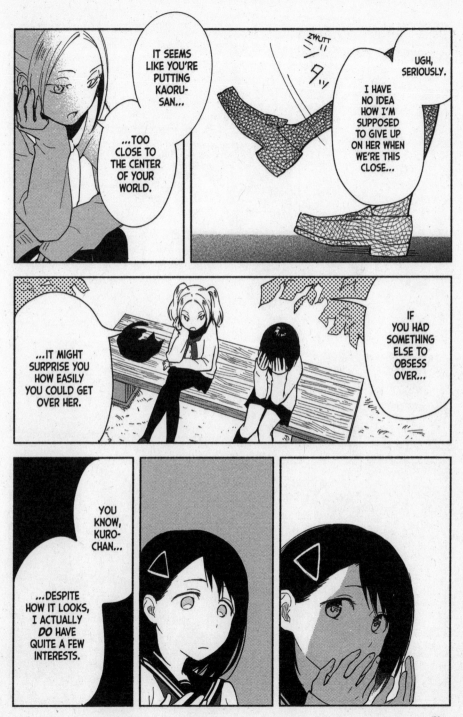

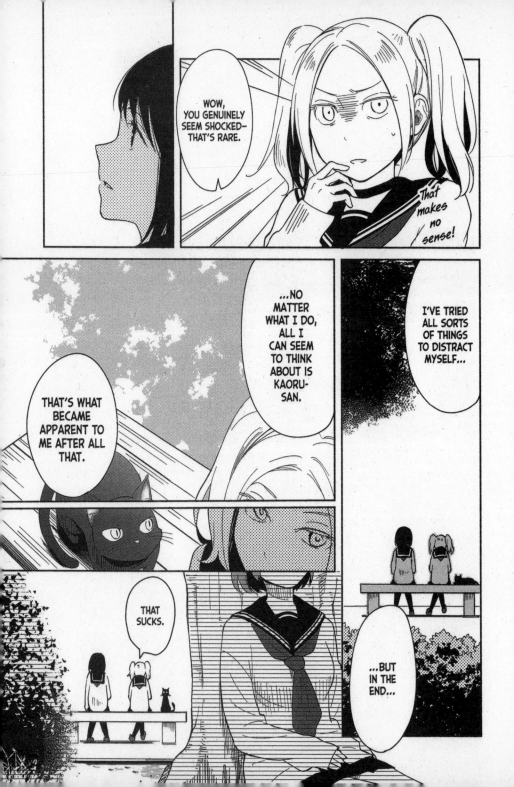

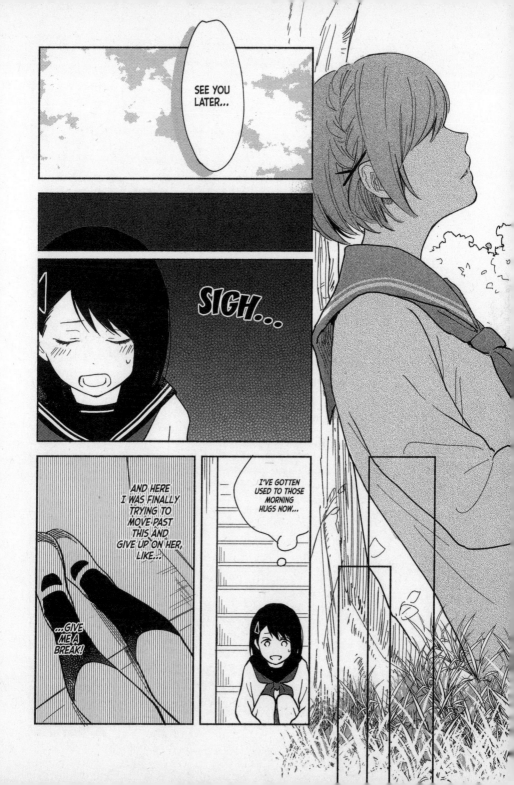

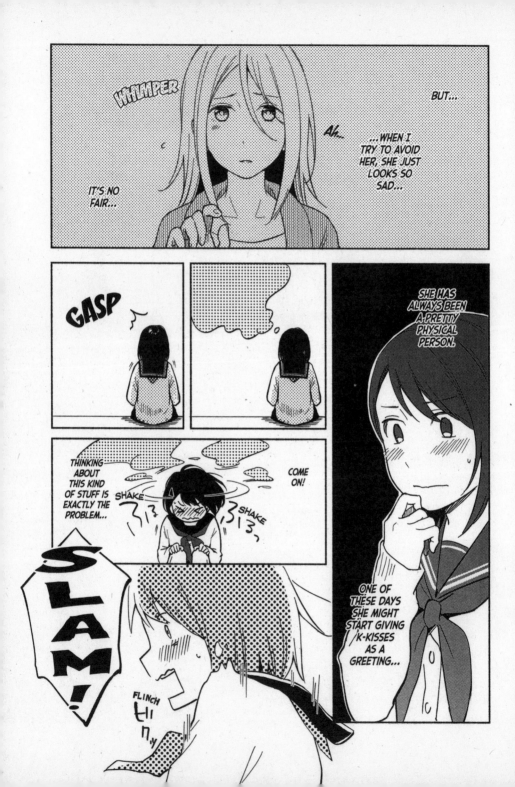

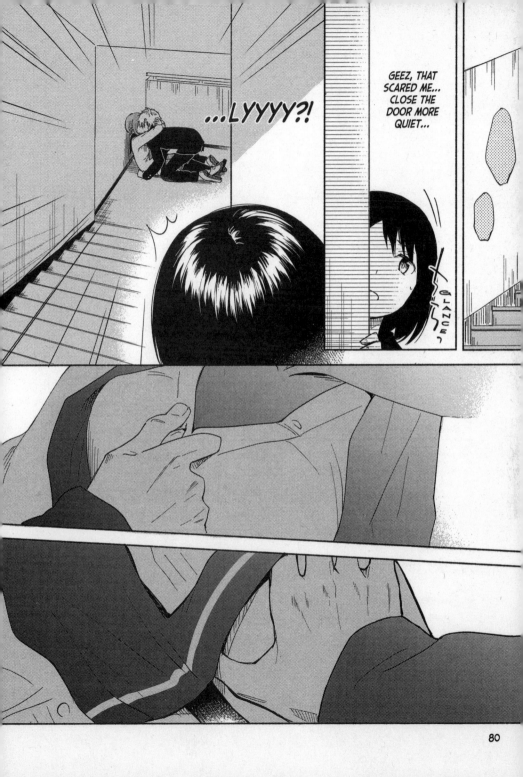

...LYYYY?!

GEEZ, THAT SCARED ME... CLOSE THE DOOR MORE QUIET...

GLANCE

WHAAA?!

WHO?!

WHA?!

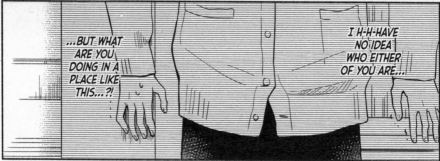

...BUT WHAT ARE YOU DOING IN A PLACE LIKE THIS...?!

I H-H-HAVE NO IDEA WHO EITHER OF YOU ARE...

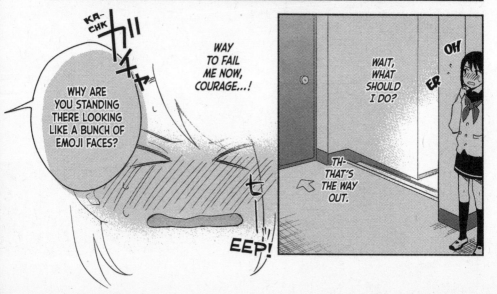

KA-CHK

WHY ARE YOU STANDING THERE LOOKING LIKE A BUNCH OF EMOJI FACES?

WAY TO FAIL ME NOW, COURAGE...!

EEP!

OH

ER

WAIT, WHAT SHOULD I DO?

TH-THAT'S THE WAY OUT.

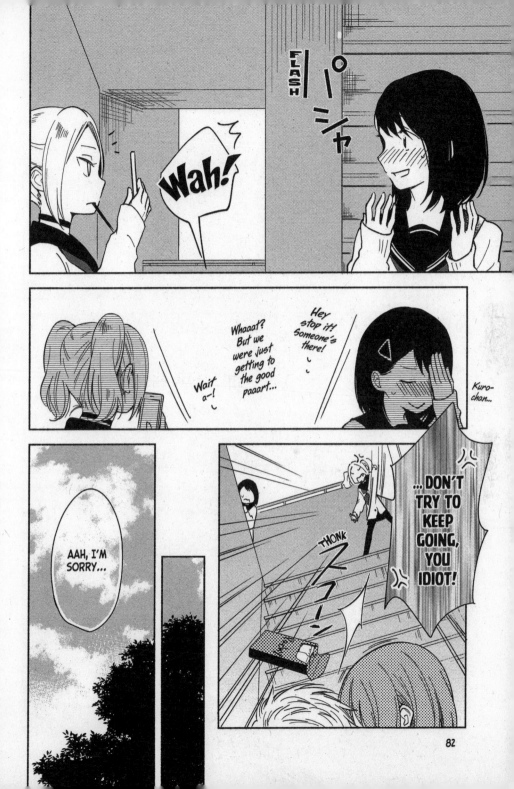

82

THROB
THROB

HM... RIGHT.

THAT'S KONATSU, SHE'S IN MY CLASS.

WE KIND OF GOT CAUGHT UP IN THE MOMENT...

AH.

A FRIEND OF YOURS?

NO, JUST AN ACQUAINTANCE.

OH! BUT...

...SHE MIGHT BE BETTER AT TALKING ABOUT ROMANCE THAN I AM.

WELL, AS YOU CAN SEE, SHE'S COMPLETELY LACKING IN COMMON SENSE...

...SO IT'S PROBABLY SAFEST YOU STAY AWAY FROM-

SHE'S FROM A COMPLETELY DIFFERENT WORLD...

SHE'S USUALLY GOT TWO OR THREE PIECES ON THE SIDE.

WH-WHA...?

SHE MAY NOT BE ALL THERE IN HER HEAD, BUT...

...AT THE VERY LEAST, SHE'S CHOCK-FULL OF EXPERIENCE.

I'VE NEVER ONCE ACTUALLY GONE OUT WITH...

...THE GUY TODAY, OR ANY OF THE PEOPLE BEFORE.

HUH?

NOW JUST A SEC, CHLOE.*

SIGH

YOU'RE GETTING IT TWISTED THERE.

IF YOU NEVER AGREED TO BE IN A CONTRACT WITH A LOVER, THEN IT ISN'T REALLY MOON-LIGHTING, NOW, IS IT?

Don't talk about it like it's a part-time job.

*IN JAPANESE, "CHLOE" IS PRONOUNCED "KUROÉ."

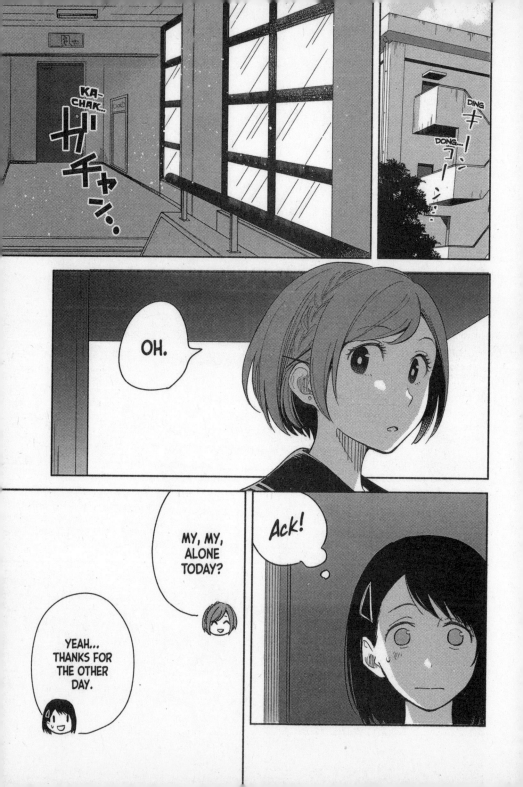

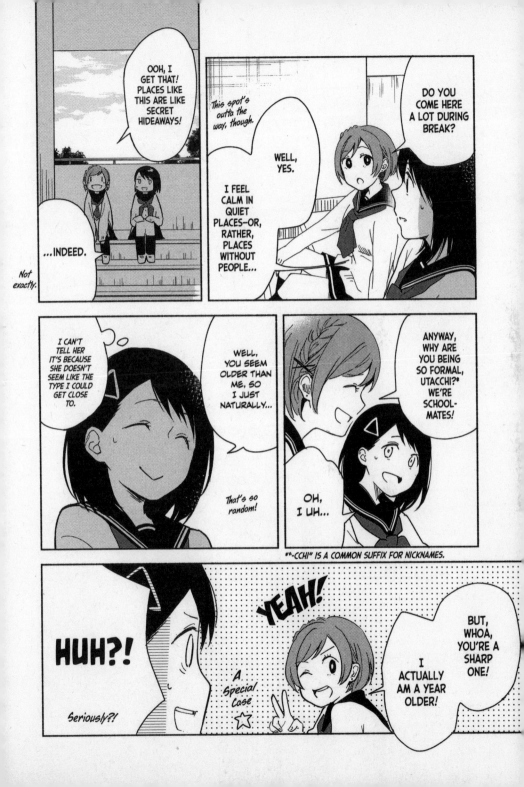

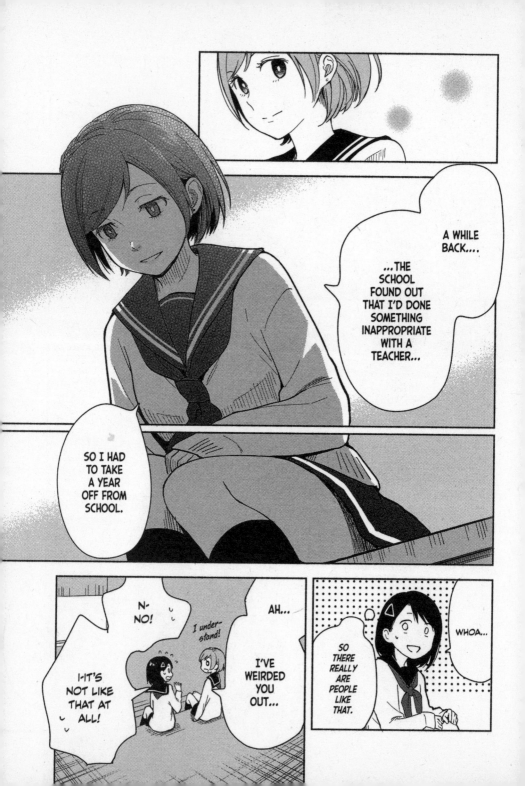

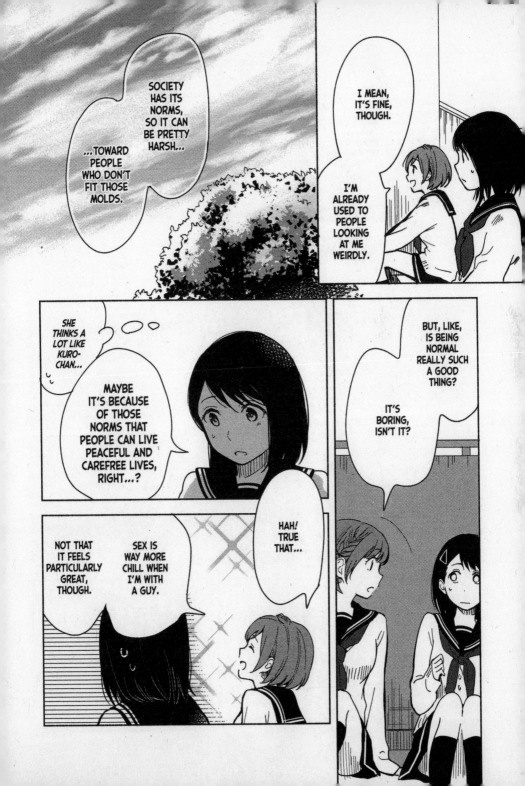

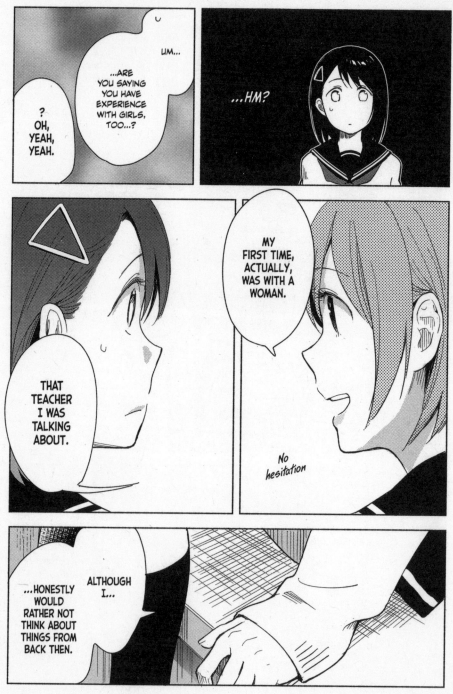

91

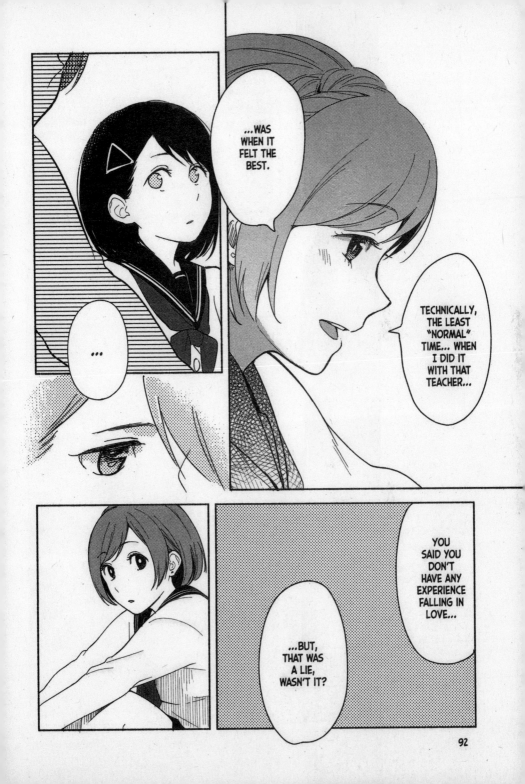

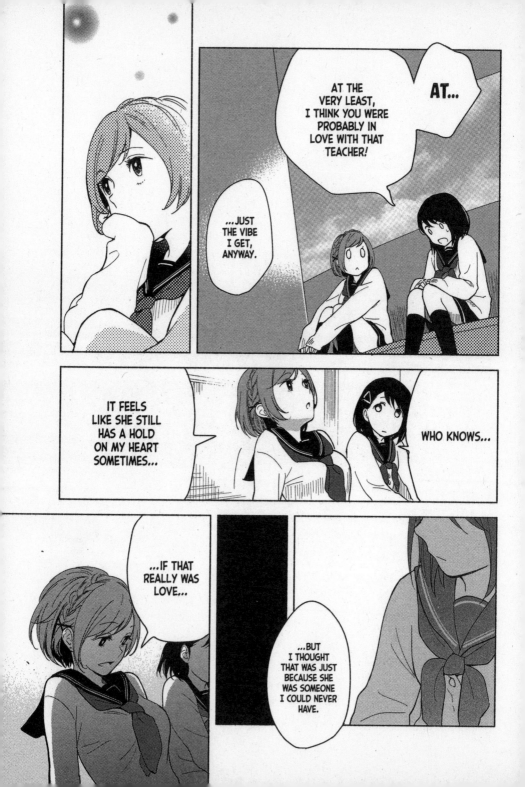

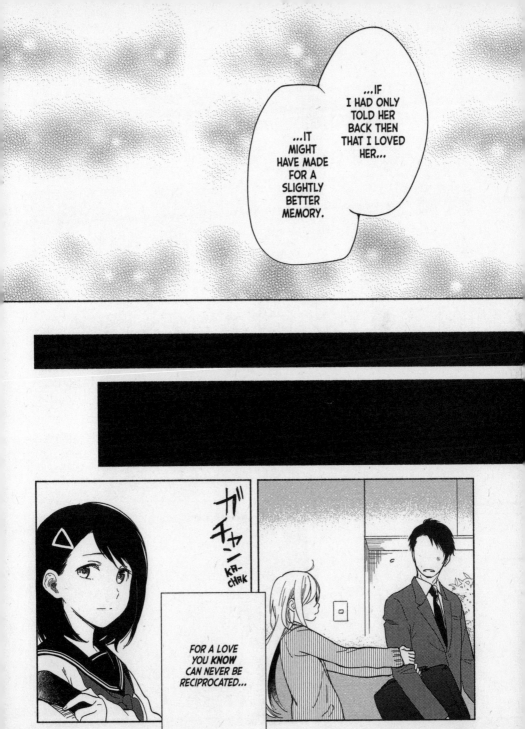

THAT NATURALLY, A DAY WOULD COME, WHEN YOUR FEELINGS FADED.

...I IMAGINED... NORMALLY, IT'D BE EASY TO GIVE UP ON.

You're still embarrassed by this?

Come on...

THAT'S WHAT I THOUGHT.

BUT WHILE WAITING FOR THAT DAY TO COME, I BEGAN TO UNDERSTAND...

UTA-CHAN...?

SQUEEZE

WHAT'S NORMAL...

...MIGHT NOT APPLY TO ME.

If I Could
Reach You

If I Could
Reach You

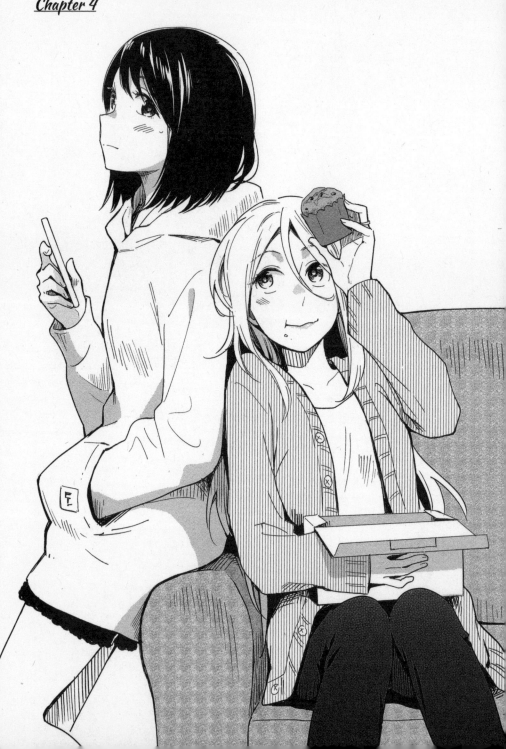

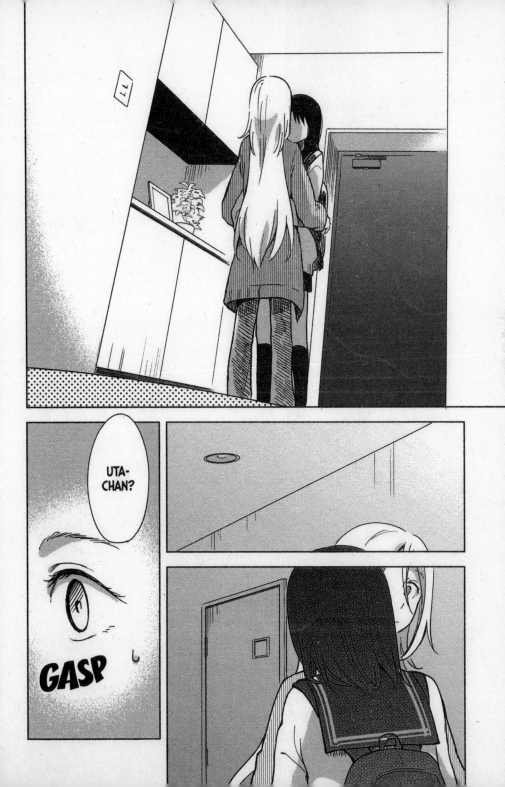

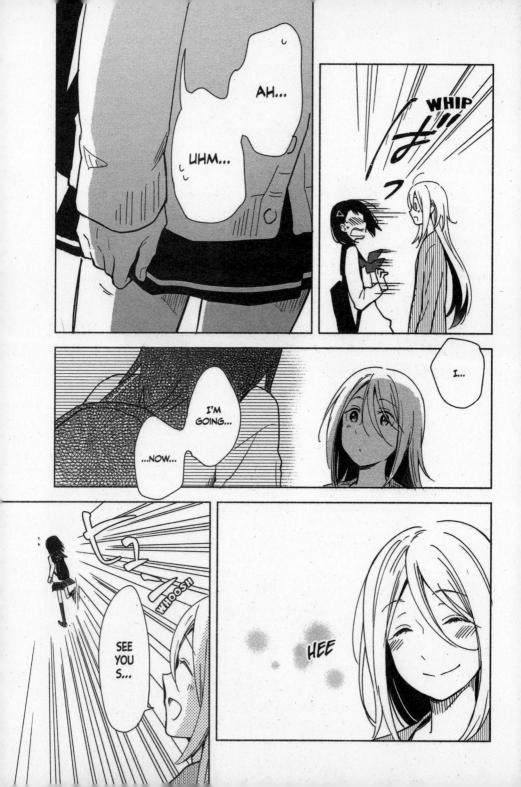

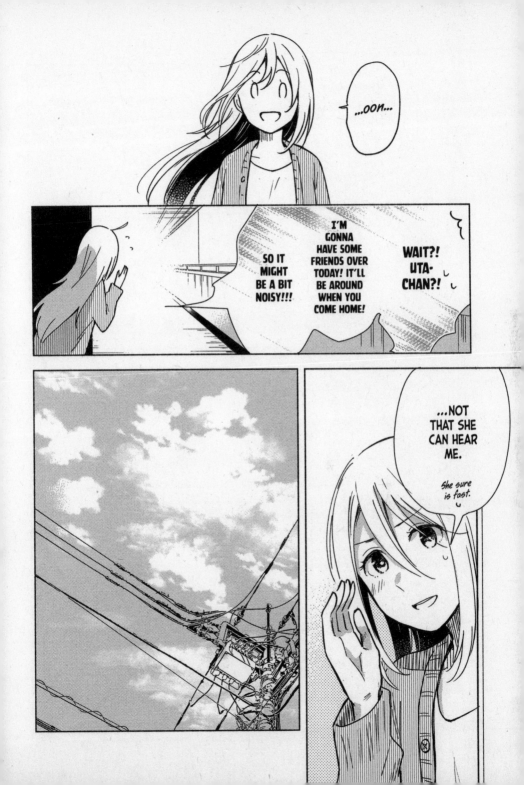

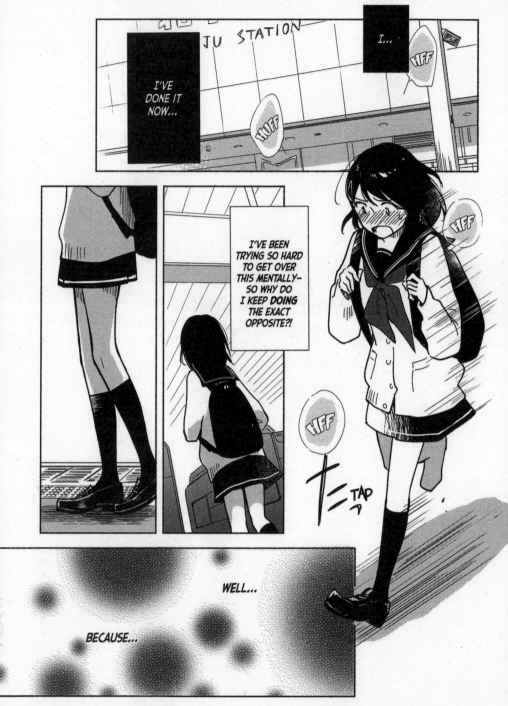

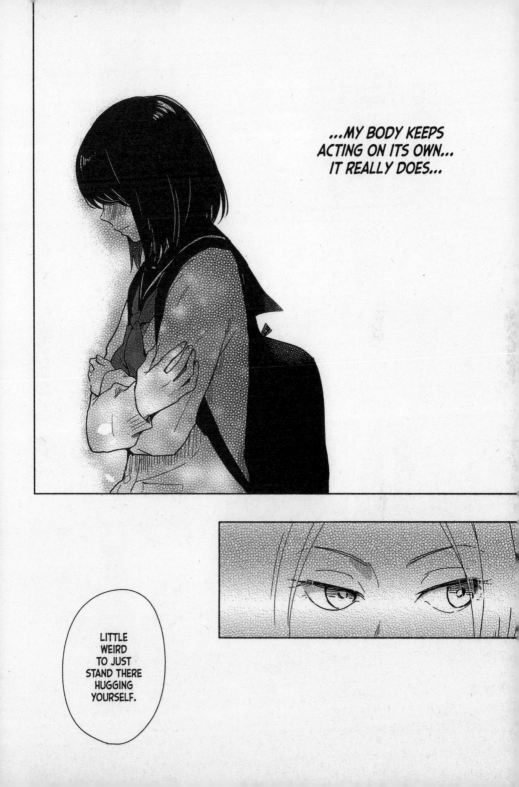

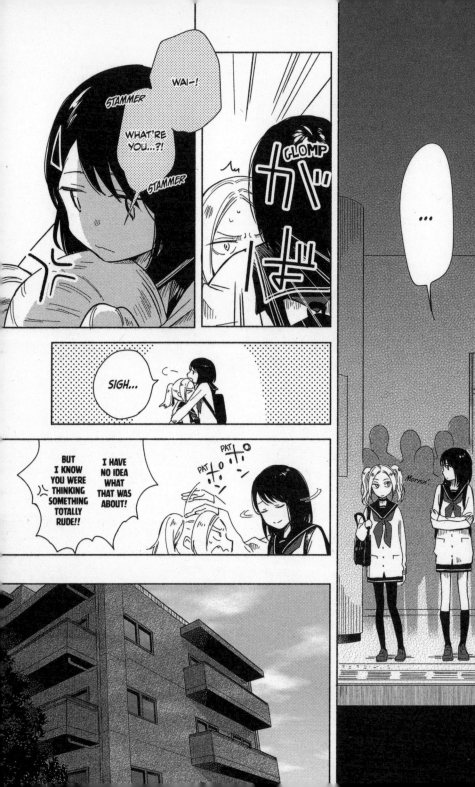

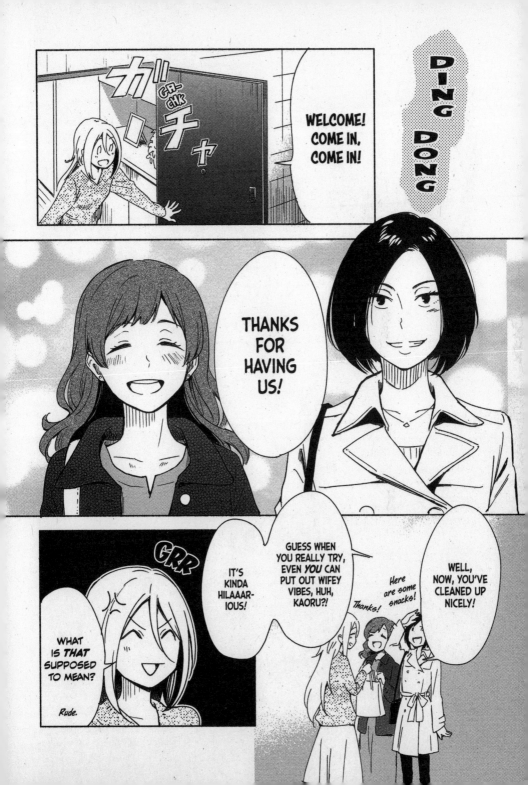

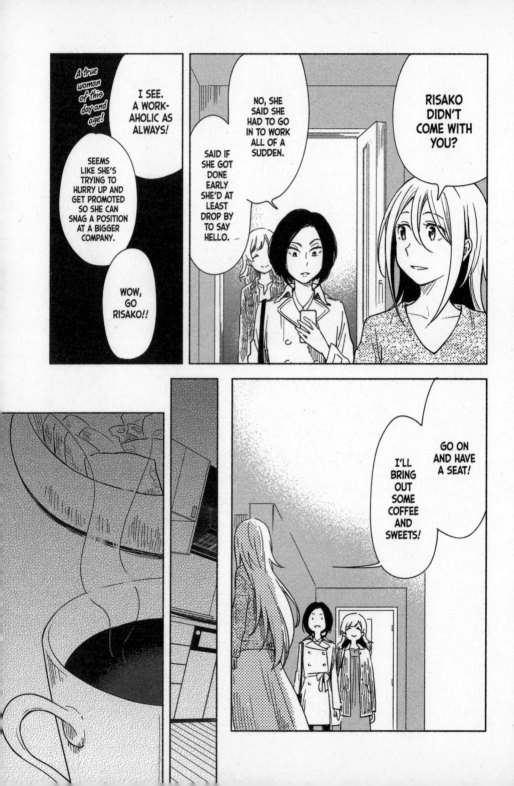

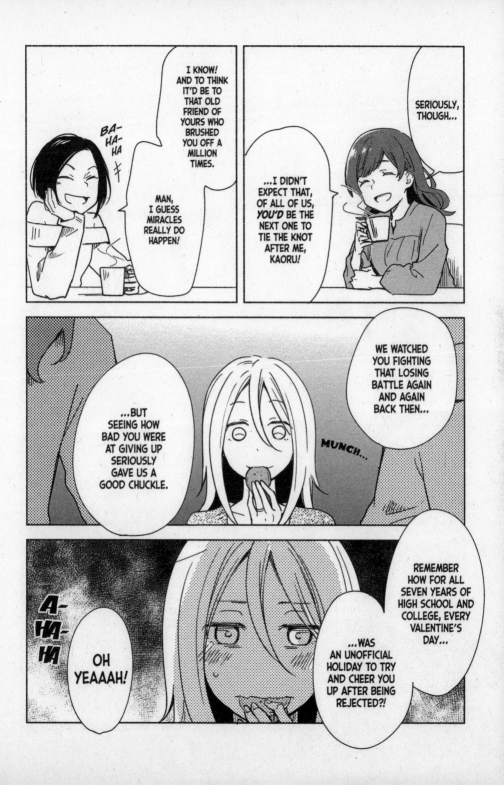

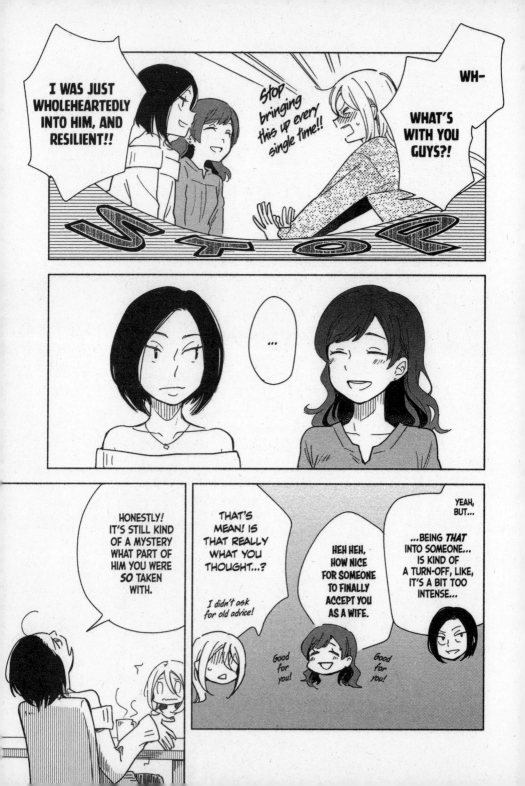

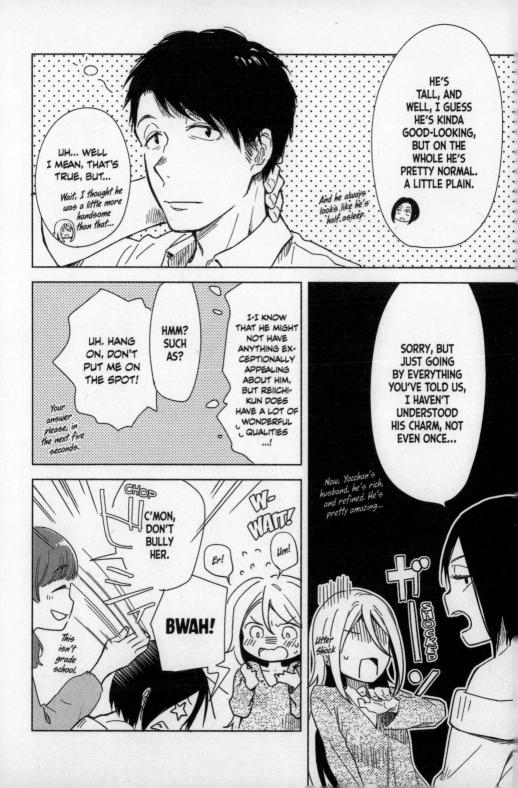

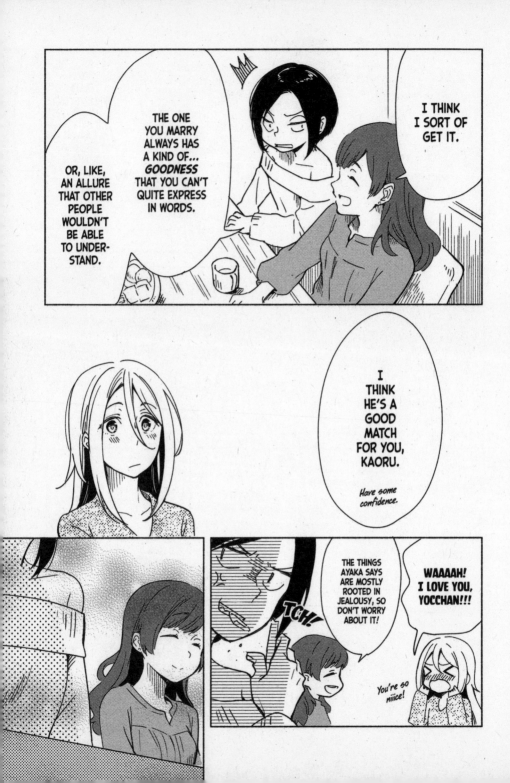

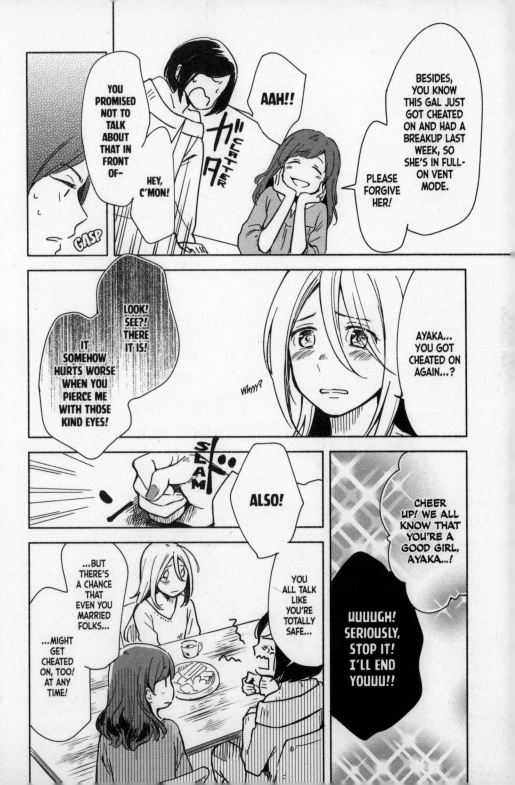

REIICHI-KUN ISN'T CAPABLE OF BEING THAT SNEAKY.

MM, I'M PRETTY SURE THERE'S NO CHANCE OF THAT HERE, EITHER, OR RATHER... IT SEEMS IMPOSSIBLE?

It's a little sad.

WHAT ABOUT YOU, KAORU?

I DON'T THINK THAT'S REALLY LIKELY WITH ME. MAYBE BECAUSE MY HUSBAND HAS ABOUT A DECADE ON ME, BUT IT FEELS LIKE HE'S STAR-STRUCK WITH ME.

SO I THINK HE'S FUNDAMENTALLY NOT GEARED TOWARD THAT...

HE CAN BE SO LAZY ABOUT EVERY-THING.

HE'S SO CARELESS, HE'S CONSTANTLY FORGETTING HIS PHONE OR WALLET.

IRK

IRK

Ah!

OH, YEAH, SHE TEXTED ME.

WHO'S THAT? RISAKO?

HM?

DING DONG

...

Quit tossin' your wedded bliss everywhere!

GRIN GRIN

YEAH, YEAH, HOW GREAT FOR THE TWO OF YOU THAT YOU'VE BAGGED YOUR-SELVES SUCH WONDERFUL HUSBANDS!

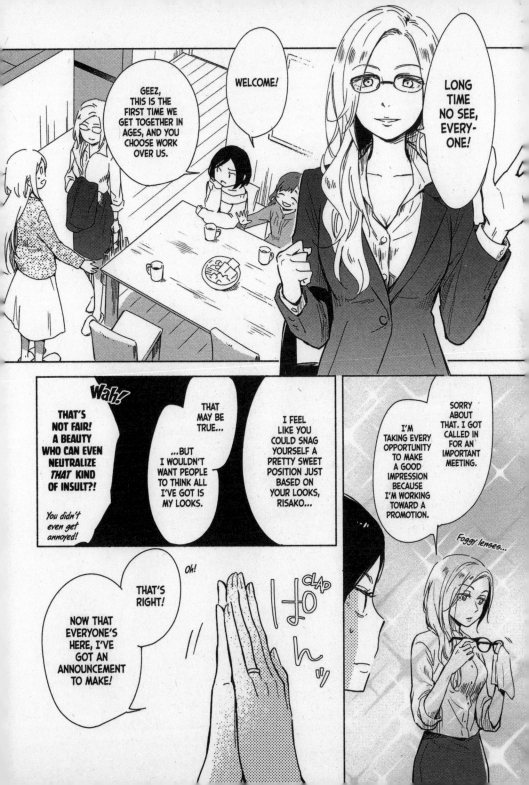

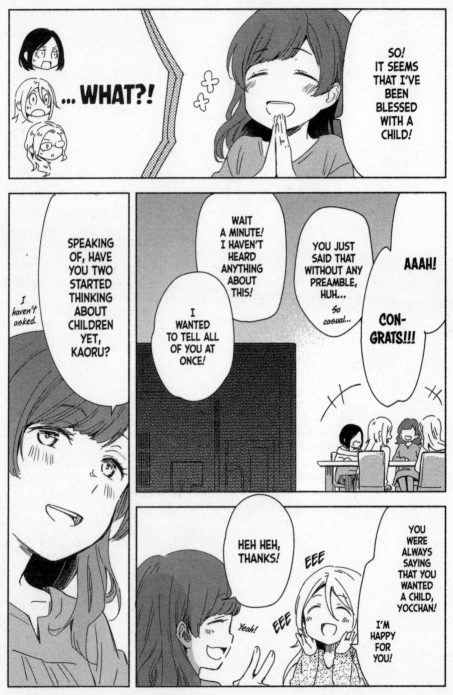

115

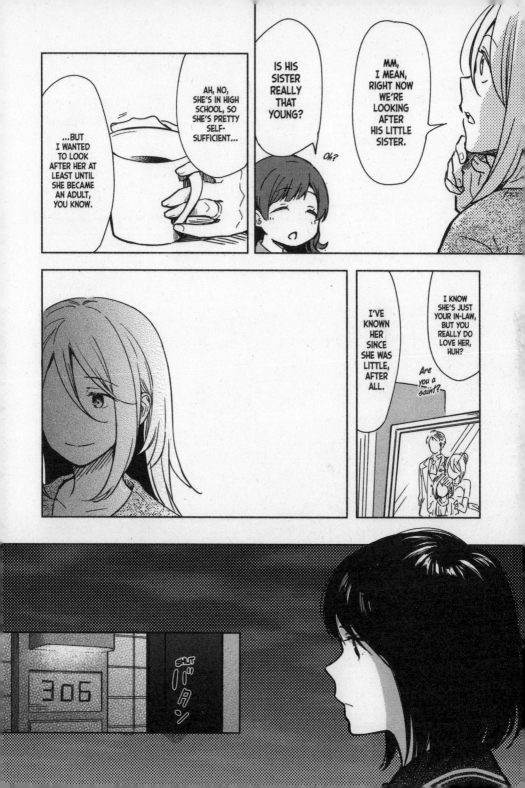

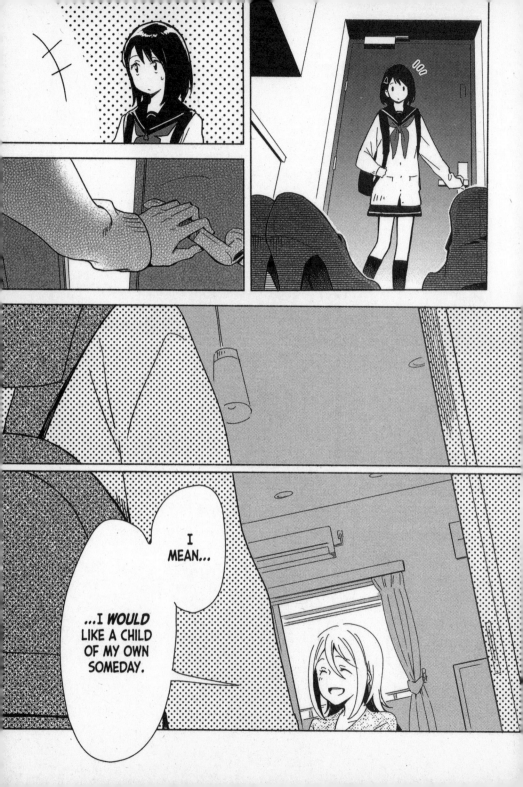

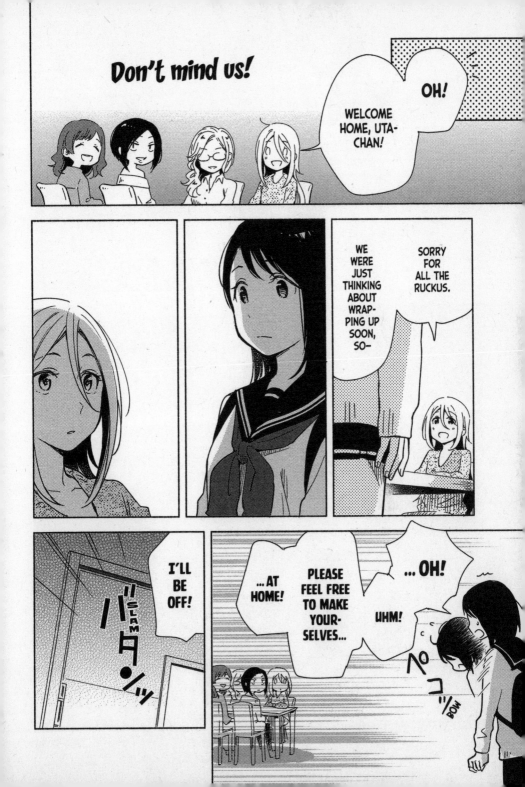

PRETTY SURE THIS IS THE FIRST I'M HEARING ABOUT THIS.

A KID... HUH?

I GUESS YOU WOULD TALK ABOUT THAT SORT OF THING WITH FRIENDS...

H... HUH?

IN OTHER WORDS...

KAORU-SAN THINKS ABOUT THESE THINGS LIKE A NORMAL PERSON...

...OR SOMETHING.

Obviously...

WHAT IS THIS FEELING?

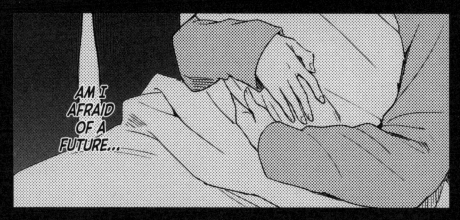

AM I AFRAID OF A FUTURE...

...WHERE KAORU-SAN WOULD BE EVEN FURTHER AWAY FROM ME THAN SHE IS NOW?

A PLACE WHERE I WOULDN'T BE ABLE TO REACH HER— FOR GOOD?

WHY AM
I STILL
HOLDING
OUT
HOPE...?

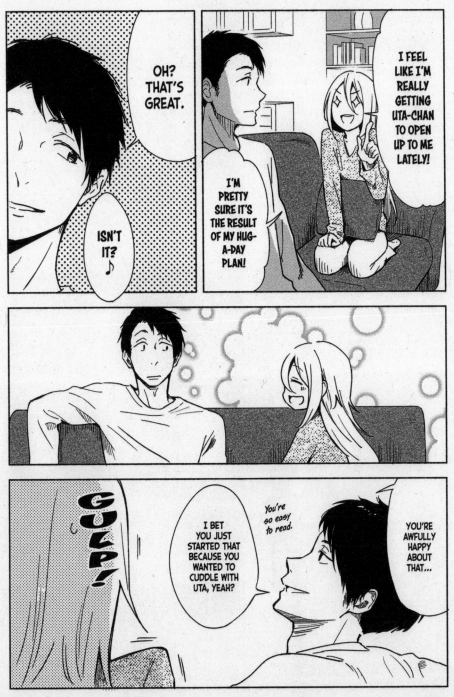

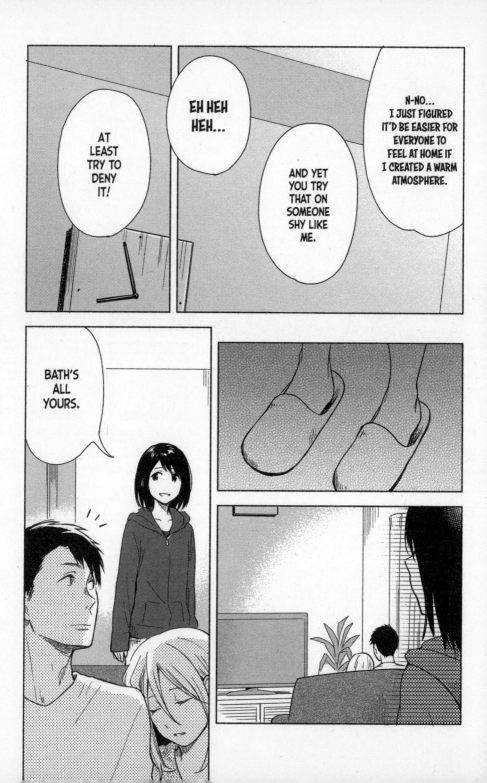

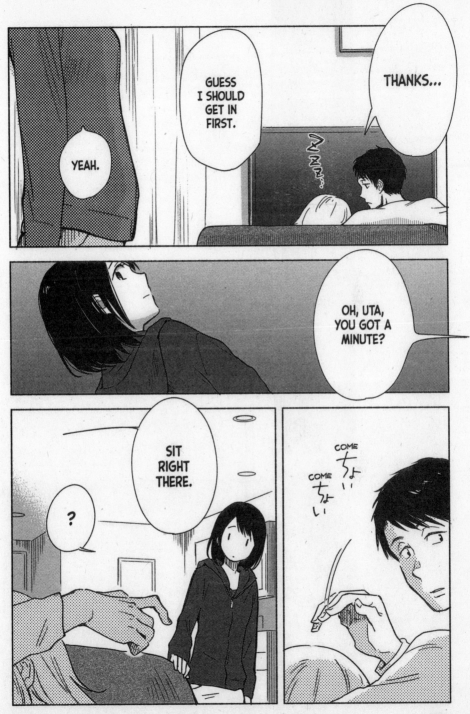

124

THMP

BATON PASS!

YOU CAN SPARE 30 MINUTES.

HEY, WAIT A-

R... REI-KUN!

I have studying to do...!

FACED WITH A LOVE I HAVE NO CHOICE BUT TO ABANDON...

I'VE TRIED SO MANY TIMES TO CONTROL MYSELF, TO DENY IT...

...IT'S OBVIOUS WHERE MY THOUGHTS TURN TO NEXT.

BUT EVERY TIME I GET A TASTE OF EVEN THE SLIGHTEST BIT OF THAT WARMTH...

"...I WANT TO FEEL MORE."

If I Could
Reach You

If I Could
Reach You

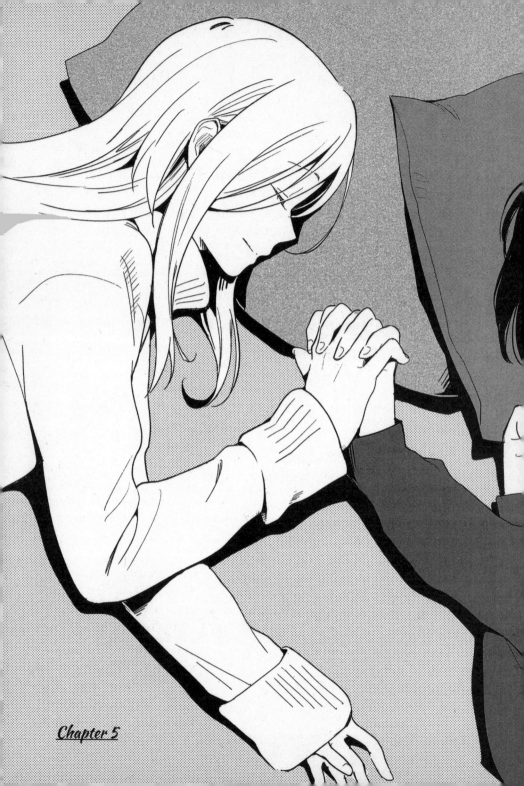

Chapter 5

PEOPLE CHANGE.
SO DO FEELINGS.

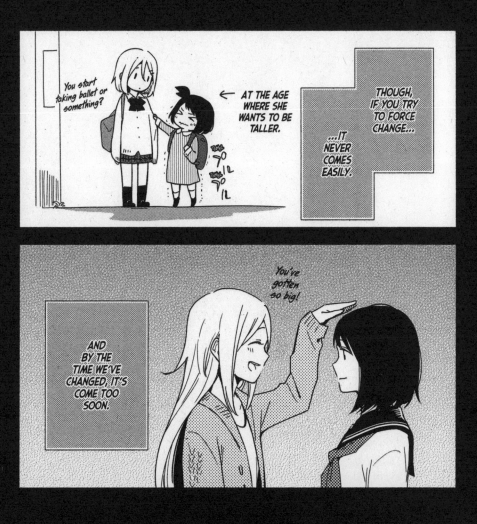

IF, BACK THEN...

...I COULD HAVE JUST...

...DONE AS I LIKED...

...THEN I WOULD'VE BEEN ABLE TO LOOK FORWARD, AND CONVEY MY FEELINGS STRAIGHT ON.

GULP...

MM...

fin.

NO WAY! I MISSED THE LAST EPISODE!!!

AW, MAN, I SHOULD HAVE SET IT TO RECORD! I'VE BEEN LOOKING FORWARD TO THIS SHOW EVERY WEEK!

FLAIL!!

UGH, LATELY I'VE JUST BEEN GETTING SO SLEEPY RIGHT AWAY!

FLAIL

ZWOOM

WAIT, HEY! WHY DIDN'T YOU WAKE ME UP, REIICHI-KUN...?

IF THE PERSON DIDN'T FEEL RIGHT, I'D HAVE WOKEN UP!

YEAH, YOU HAVE THE SAME... AURA? OR VIBE? IT'S SOMETHING LIKE...A COMFORTING FEELING.

HUH? SIMILAR?

HA, YOU'RE KINDA SIMILAR, SO I DIDN'T REALIZE...

OH?

YOU'RE HERE NOW, UTA-CHAN...

...When'd that happen?

I... SEE.

AHA-HA...

...GOOD NIGHT.

I'M GONNA HEAD BACK TO MY ROOM.

WELL, LATER, THEN.

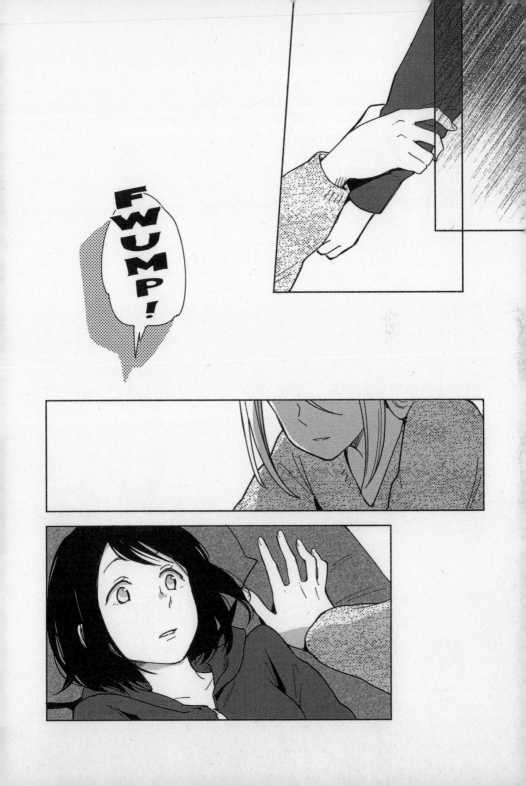

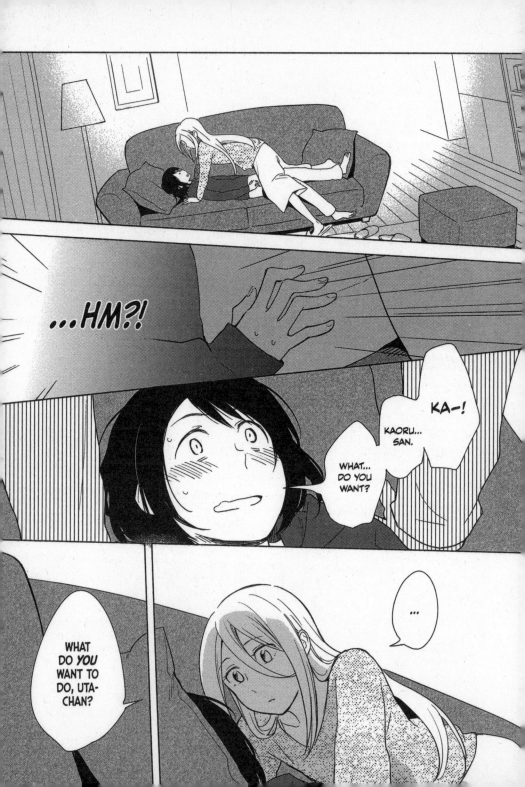

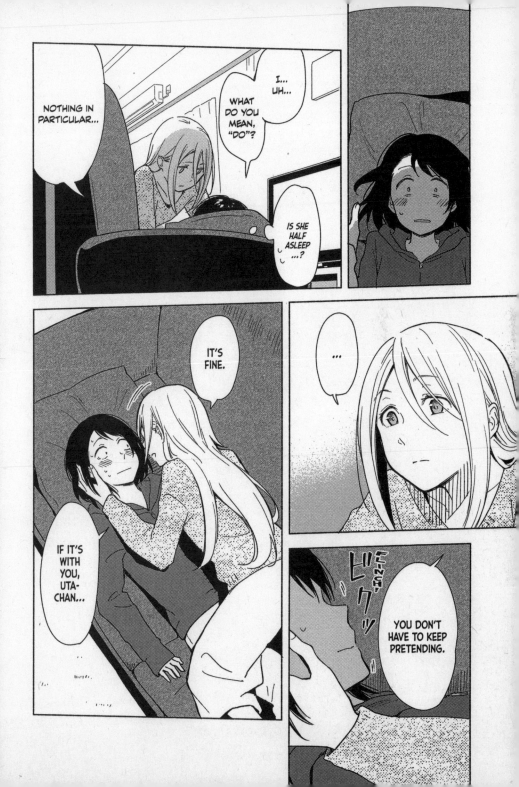

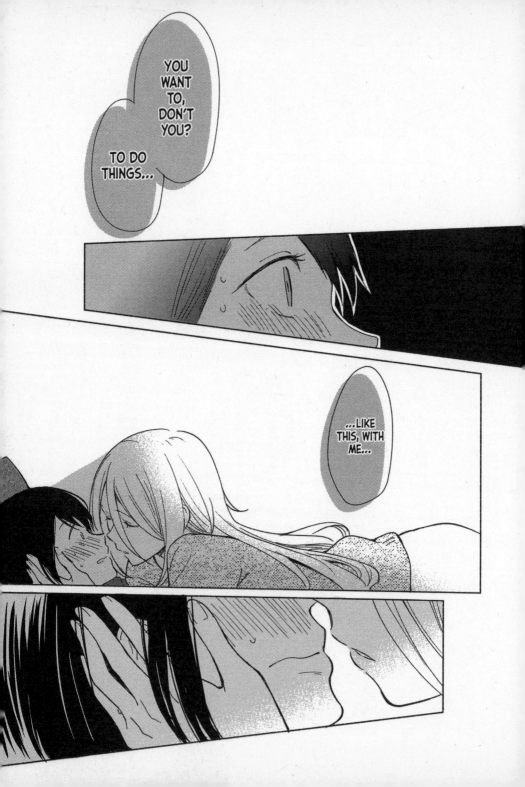

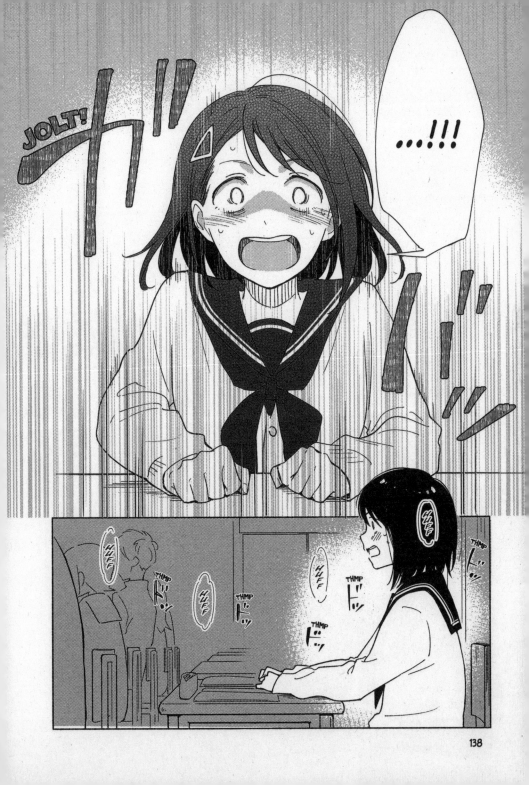

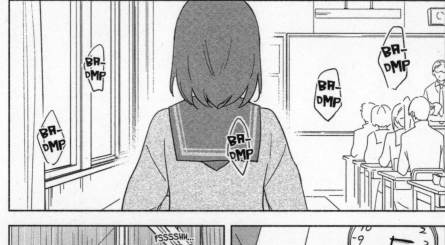

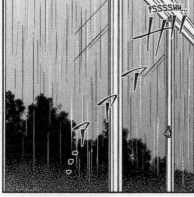

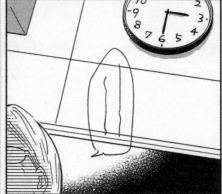

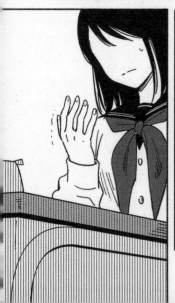

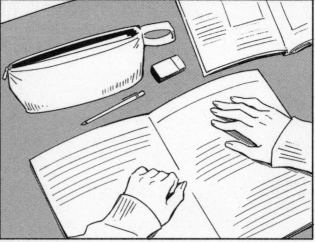

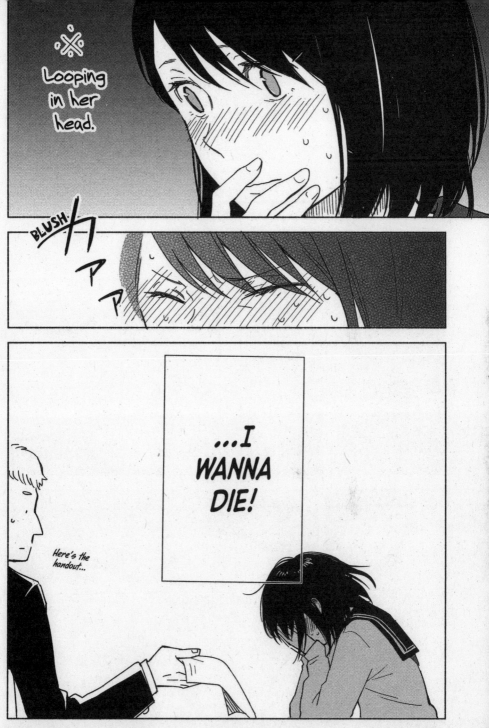

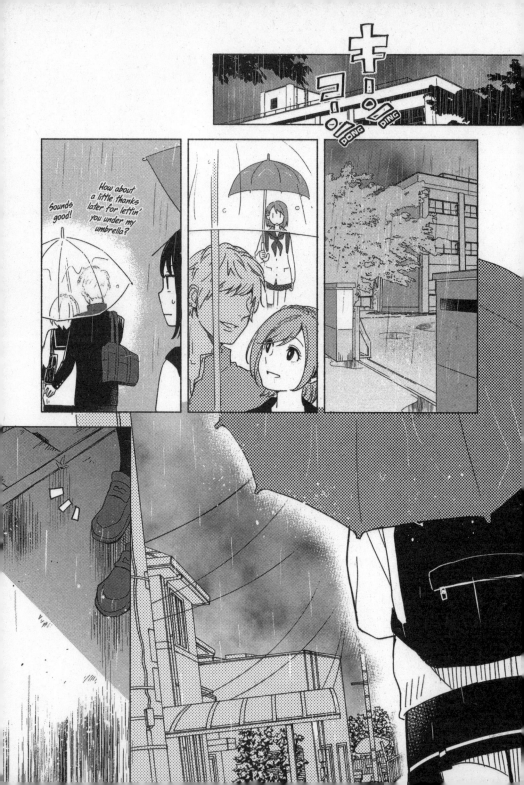

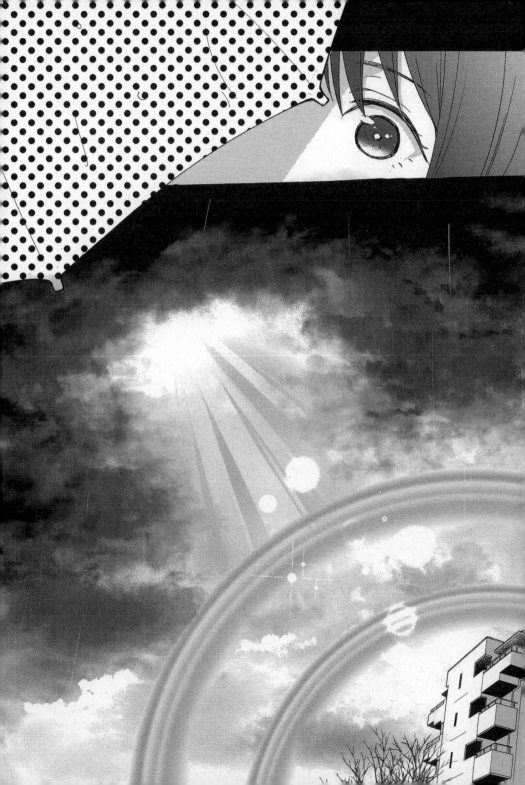

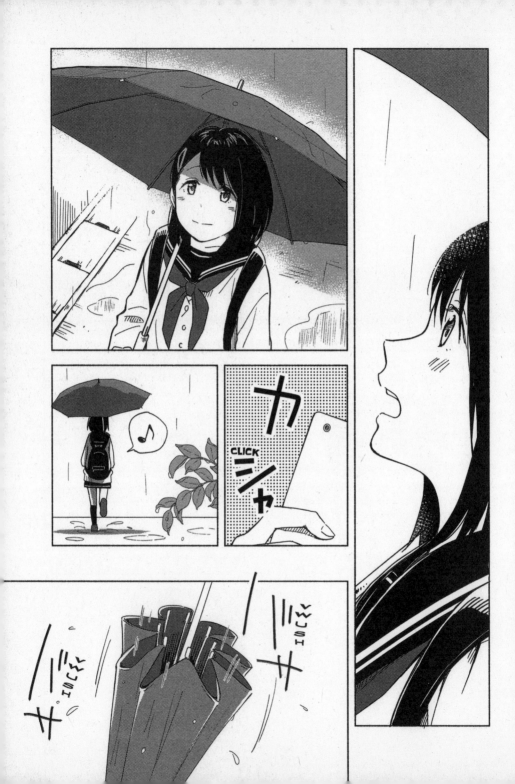

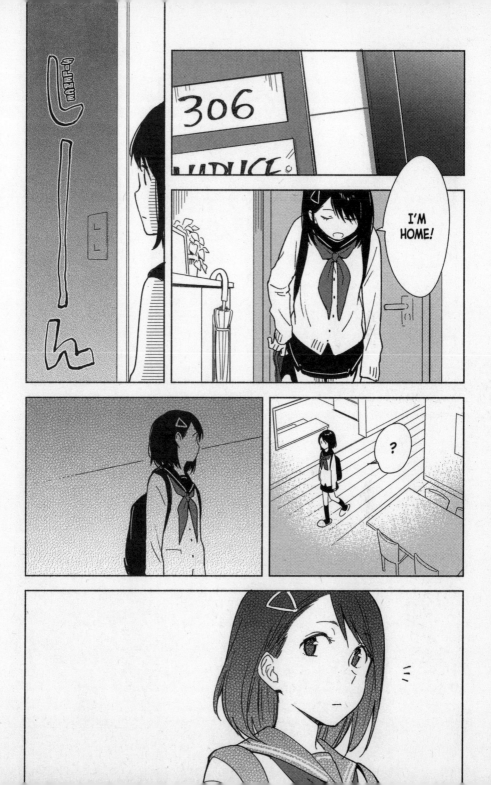

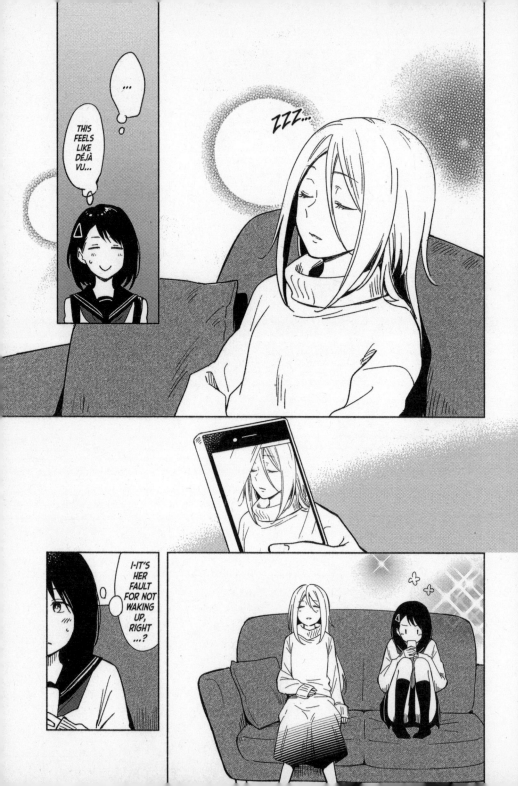

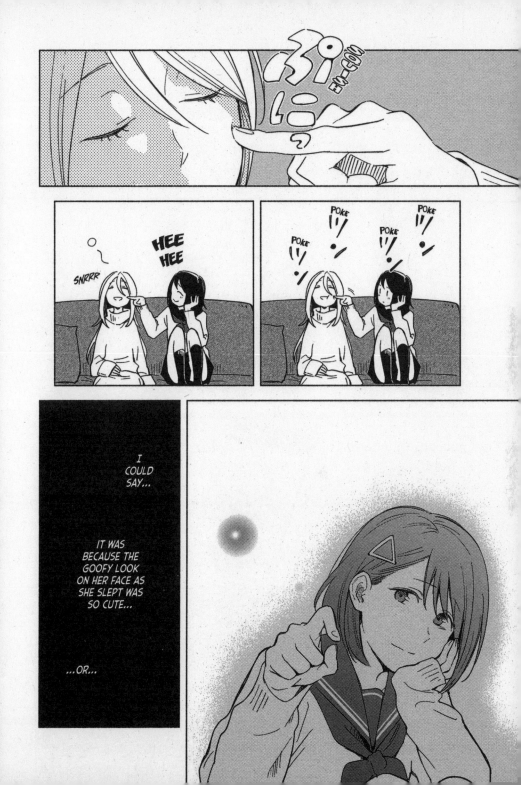

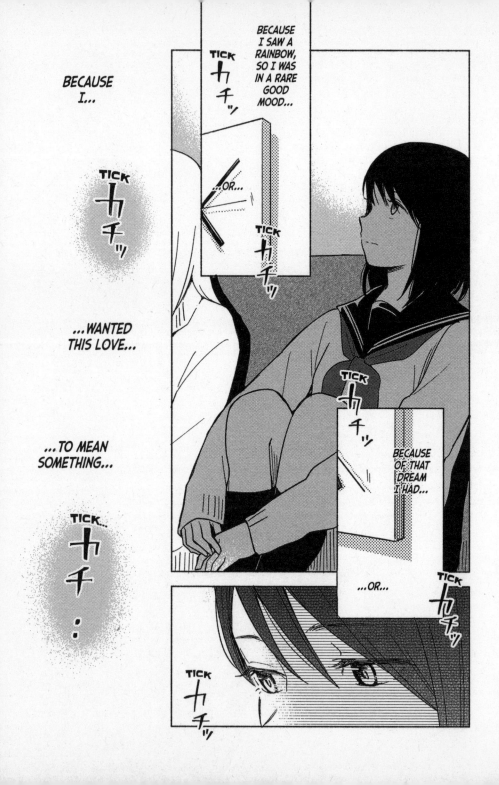

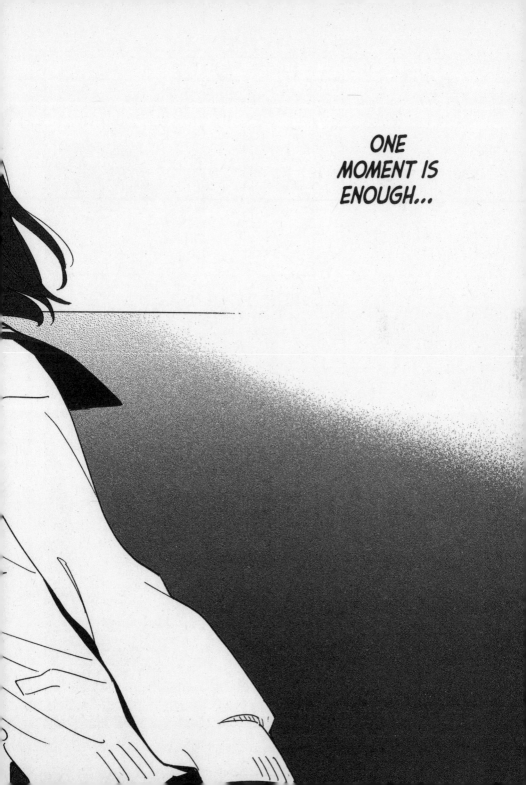

ONE
MOMENT IS
ENOUGH...

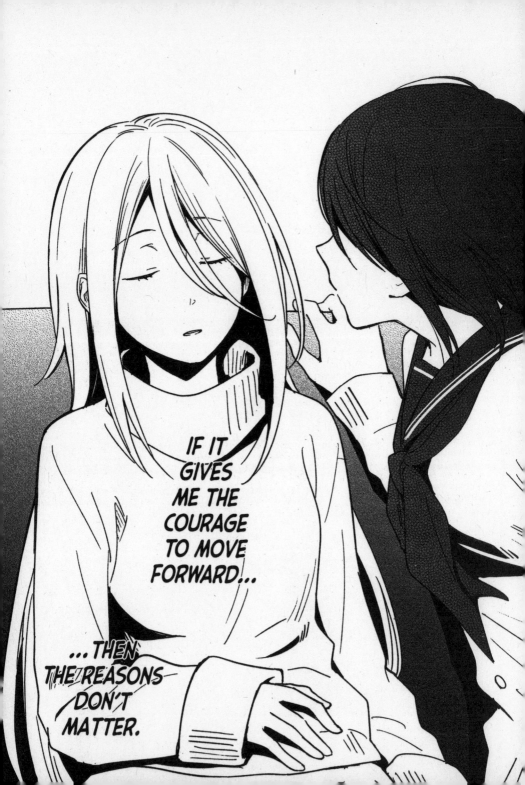

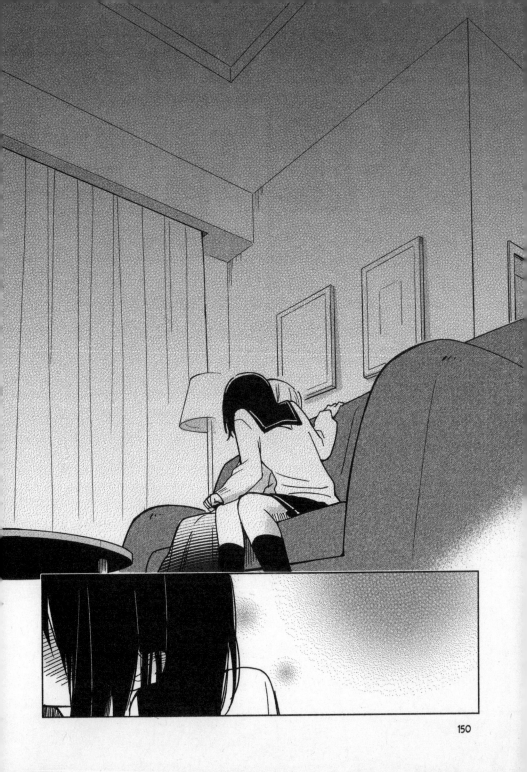

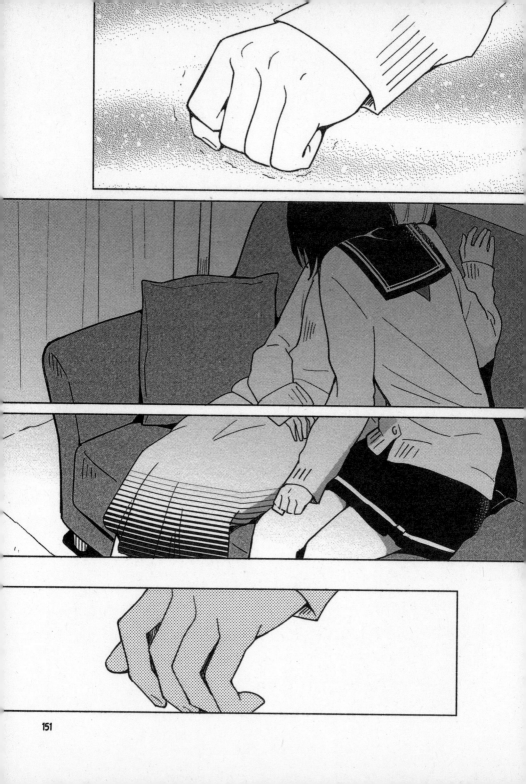

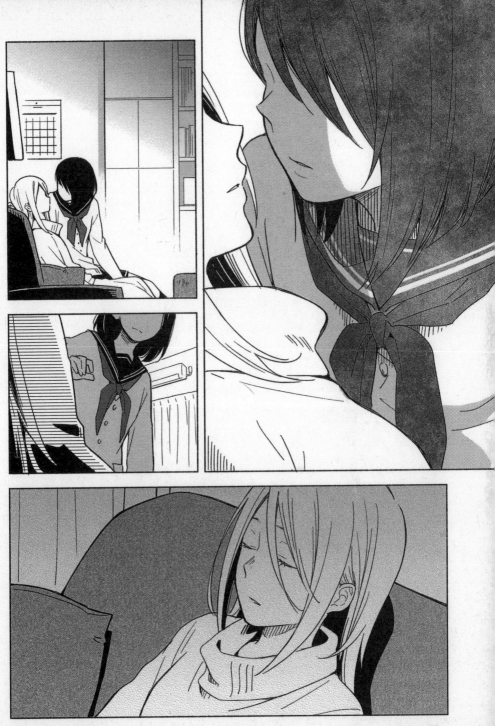

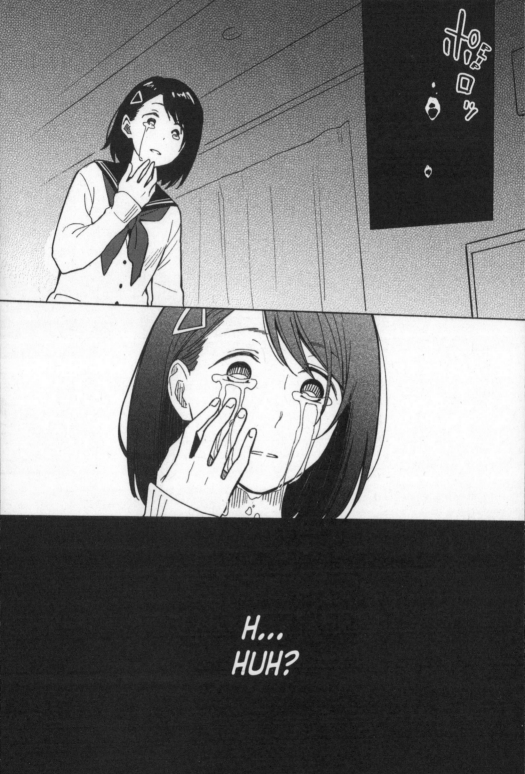

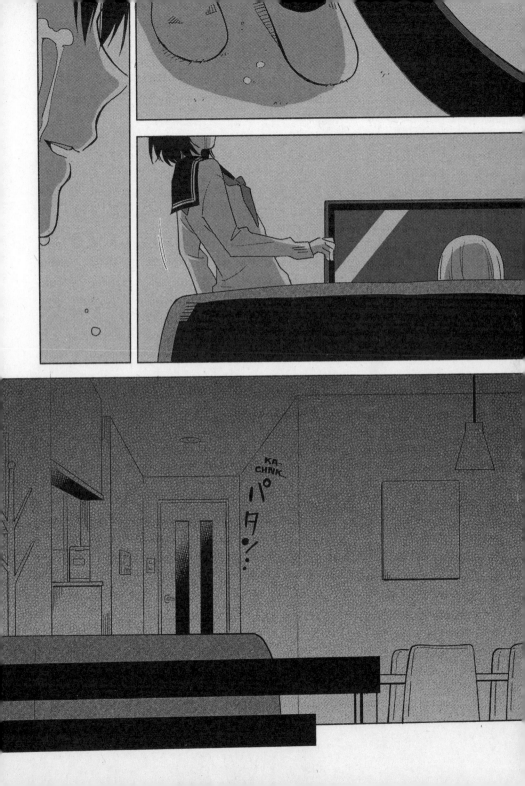

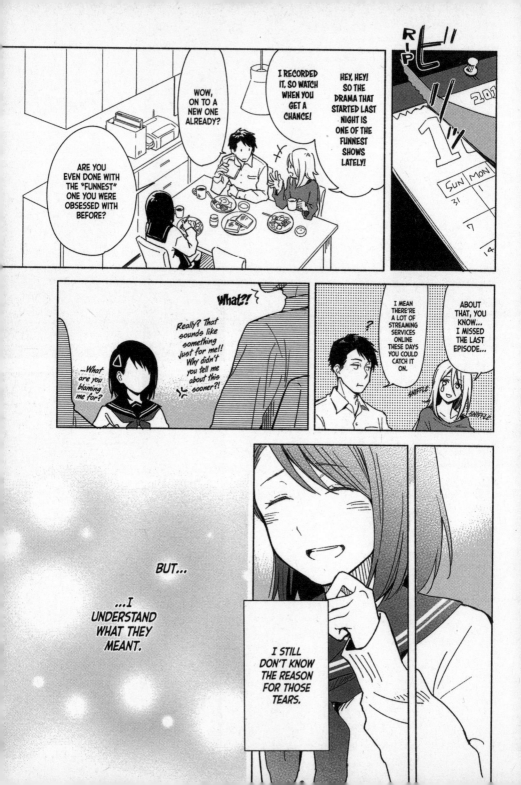

MY
FIRST CRUSH
WAS OVER
TOO SOON—
LIKE THE
FINALE OF SOME
DRAMA THAT
PASSED ME BY.

To be continued.

If I Could Reach You

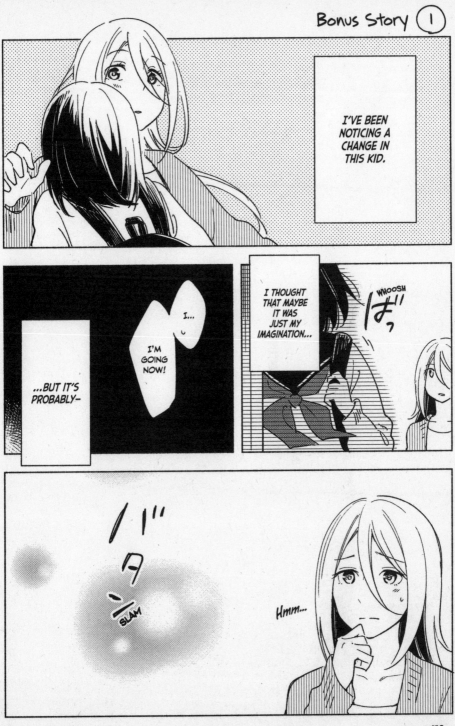

End

*ISOFLAVONE IS A COMPOUND FOUND IN SOYBEANS THOUGHT TO INCREASE ESTROGEN PRODUCTION.

IF YOU SWAPPED INTO SOMEONE ELSE'S BODY, I'D THINK SOMEONE WOULD FIGURE IT OUT RIGHT AWAY.

Movie Book

WHAAAT?

And I mean, it's fiction, anyway.

JUST LIKE YOU.

YEAH, BUT ALL THE HUMANS AROUND ARE STUPID, RIGHT?

IF IT WAS SOMEONE CLOSE TO ME, I'M SURE THAT I WOULD REALI...

You're so mean...

Hm?

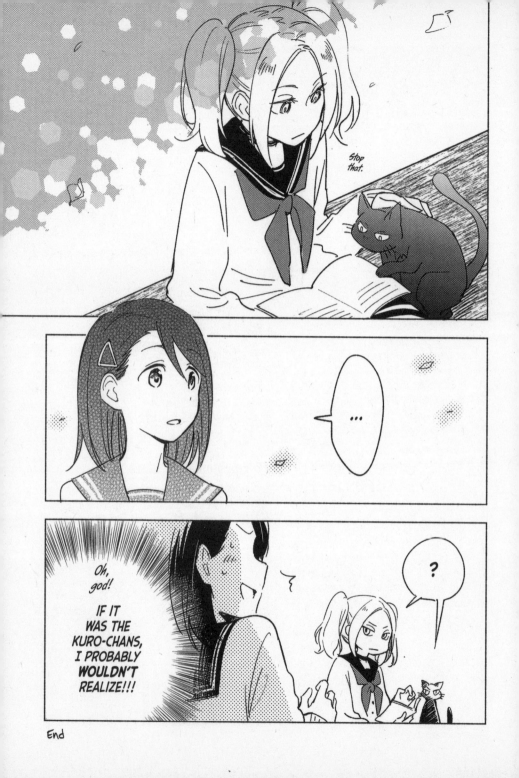

End

Afterword
by tMnR (Tomonori)

I'd like to extend my deepest gratitude to you for purchasing volume 1 of If I Could Reach You. I hope that you've enjoyed it.

My thanks...

BOW

BOW

Hello and greetings! I am tMnR, a.k.a. Tomonori.

Naturally, this is my first ever afterword, too, so I thought I'd give a bit of self-introduction, combined with a bit of my process, or something like that...

...but, well, how do I put this? There isn't much to say!!

I've only drawn doujin...*

Hmm...

RUMMMBLE

...so I'm still a bit flustered by all the praise...

Goodness, it's the door to an unknown world...

This book marks my first collected volume, and my commercial debut...

*FAN-MADE COMICS OR MAGAZINES.

Nothing Inside

POP

I'm so sorry...

I've always been a carefee person, jumping from one interest to the next.

Ahahahaha! Now I'll float over there!

FWUFF FWUFF

Mostly because... I never really yearned to be a mangaka.

Before the Deadline

ZZZ

I would be so glad for your continued support from here on, too!

See you!

It was hard, but I'm glad I tried it... It was stressful, but fun.

...So, well, imagine turning a lax author like that into a serious one—now that's something I hope I "Could Reach."

Special Thanks

Editor Saito-san
Designer-san
Everyone Else Involved
and my Dearest Readers

A Kodansha Comics Trade Paperback Original
If I Could Reach You volume 1 copyright © 2017 tMnR
English translation copyright © 2019 tMnR

Published in the United States by Kodansha Comics, an imprint of
Kodansha USA Publishing, LLC, New York.

Publication rights for this English edition arranged through
Kodansha Ltd, Tokyo.

First published in Japan in 2017 by Ichijinsha Inc., Tokyo,
as *Tatoe Todokanu Itodatoshitemo* volume 1

ISBN 978-1-63236-887-4

Printed in the United States of America.

www.kodanshacomics.com

9 8 7 6 5 4 3 2 1
Translation: Diana Taylor
Lettering: Jennifer Skarupa
Editing: Haruko Hashimoto
Kodansha Comics edition cover design by Phil Balsman